Ivan Sinclair 2005

DOUBLE DECK TROLLEYBUSES OF THE WORLD

beyond the British Isles

by Brian Patton

Published by Adam Gordon

Cover illustrations

Front Cover:
Pontevadra: No.5 passes Pastora en route to Marin on 30 August 1968.

Back Cover:
Left to right:
Cape Town No.101 heading into the city on Service 8 on 7 June 1957.
Santander-Astillero: T87 leaving Tarragona on 10 September 1968.
Durban: On the last morning of trolleybus service no.2068 is seen at the junction of Battle Road and Stellawood Road in Umbilo.
Adelaide: No.428 at Hackney depot about 1956.

A catalogue entry for this book is available from the British Library.

ISBN : 1874422508

Publication no. 52

Edition limited to 700 copies

Published by
Adam Gordon
Kintradwell Farmhouse,
Brora,
Sutherland
KW9 6LU

Tel: 01408 622660
E-mail: adam@adamgordon.freewire.co.uk

Printed in 2004 by The Launton Press, Bicester, Oxon

Typesetting and design by Trevor Preece, trevor@epic.gb.com

CONTENTS

DOUBLE DECK TROLLEYBUSES OF THE WORLD
beyond the British Isles

INTRODUCTION

Following on from the study of double-deck trams which have operated in countries beyond the British Isles, it seemed that it would be worthwhile considering double-deck trolleybuses which have also run outwith these islands. In the event, this has proved to be a much simpler study than that on trams, since with one exception, the history of the double-deck trolleybus abroad (as viewed from Britain) has been almost entirely a British story. The trolleybus flourished in the years when it was flourishing in Britain and declined when it was declining at home, though the last to run (in Porto) outlived the last British operation by almost a quarter of a century. Very many of the vehicles were of typically British design and many were fitted out with the same care as were home models in the 1930s. Even where the trolleybuses were actually built in the country in which they would run, they were in almost all cases based on British designs, in the case of Barcelona that design being that of a petrol-electric motorbus. Two batches were constructed in Italy, for Porto and Johannesburg, but they were of British appearance. In the former case, the order probably went to Italy because no British manufacturer was then willing to supply double-deckers, and in the case of the latter were simply a twin design of that prepared by Sunbeam, the order going to Italy because the British firm was unable to deliver the total number of vehicles required. Only in Germany were completely new designs prepared, but the numbers were so small that they had no influence on later developments, either in their home country or elsewhere. None of the world's trolleybus systems now run double-deckers, but it is good to know that quite a few have been preserved and details of these are given in each chapter.

The book is divided by continents, with details of each operation given separately. In the case of a few systems, such as Bloemfontein and Colombo, which have not been the subject of a book or longer journal article, and are not likely to be in the foreseeable future, more information is given than is strictly necessary to cover the double-decker story. In the interests of completeness, some details are also given of single-deckers in those fleets, with a few illustrations, and there is a brief account of two pioneer systems in South Africa which did not use double-deckers. For the majority of systems, however, the reader is referred for further information to other published works, as detailed in the bibliography at the end of each section. However, mention should be made here of one source which has been used in the preparation of the entire book:

World Trolleybus Encyclopaedia. Alan Murray
Trolleybooks, Reading, 2000

Tables at the end of the book detail total numbers of vehicles which operated, and also exports from Britain and other countries.

Certain terms used require further explanation. A few place names have changed since trolleybus days. Ceylon is now Sri Lanka, but the former designation is used as it was current throughout the trolleybus period. Lourenço Marques is now Maputo, but the former name is used for the same reason. Much more recently, long after the last trolleybus ran,

Durban has become Tekweni and San Sebastian has become Domostia. Bilbao is now often referred to by its Basque name of Bilbo, although both usages are still current.

Terms such as "European", as used in South Africa in the days of apartheid are, where used, placed in quotation marks, as a matter of historical record and are not part of the vocabulary of this book.

Given the British ancestry of most of the vehicles described here, the imperial system of measurement has been used, except in the case of trolleybuses operating in countries which used the metric system, in which case both measurements are given. Vehicle capacities, such as 30/26, show the upper deck seating over that of the lower deck.

It would not have been possible to have compiled this book without the help extended so willingly by so many people in both Britain and other countries, as follows:

For provision of photographs, I am grateful to Pam Eaton, London; James Smith and Les Pivnic, Johannesburg; Peter Haseldine, Essex; Caroline Gould, Museum of English Rural Life, University of Reading; John Grant-Silver, Ayrshire; Bruce Jenkins, Faversham; David Jones, New Zealand; Kevan Mardon, Durban; Messrs Müller und Ley, Würzbach; Alan Murray, Horsham; Noel Reed, Hornsby New South Wales; Dr John Radcliffe, Glen Osmond, South Australia; Lars Richter, Hamburg; Alexander Sharin, Moscow; Peter Waller, Ian Allan Ltd., Surrey; John Whitehead, Reading; Fred York, DTS Publishing; Vic Solomons, Sydney.

Much useful information on Colombo was given by Douglas Beath, Burnie, Tasmania, and Alexander Sharin and Sergei Tarkhov, Moscow, contributed interesting information on that system. Ross Willson, Canberra, along with Garth Evans and Chris Steele, Adelaide, went to great trouble to ensure that the Australian section is a correct record of the operations in Sydney and Adelaide, and their assistance in this is much appreciated. Others who have helped are Graham Bilbe, Roland Box and John Whitehead, all of Reading; Michael Davis, DTS Publishing, Croydon; Martin Jenkins, Walton-on-Thames; Geoff Lumb, Huddersfield, John Shearman, Tunbridge Wells and John Ward, Sydney.

As always, Rosy Thacker, former librarian, National Tramway Museum, Crich, was an invaluable source of information and references and gave much help in suggesting possible leads on the more obscure systems.

I am especially grateful to Mrs Ruth Kerr of Wellington, New Zealand, for so readily granting permission to use material taken and written by her father, the late Roger Perry, who did so much to make many enthusiasts, including myself, welcome on visits to South Africa. Her former neighbour in Scotland, Janet Stirling, who kindly put us in touch, has also to be thanked for her help in making the contact.

It will be obvious that the quality of some of the illustrations is below standard. The choice of all the pictorial material was entirely mine, and these particular views have been included because of their intrinsic interest and their rarity.

Foulden, Berwickshire.
August 2004.

SOUTHERN AFRICA

BLOEMFONTEIN

The capital of the Orange Free State was, after Germiston and Boksburg, the third city in South Africa to inaugurate trolleybuses, on 16 December 1915. It was then a small city of only 15,000 population. Despite the undertaking's title of "Municipal Tramways", trams, although promised by the Council on several occasions, had not been introduced, and the trolleybuses were its first vehicles. There were ultimately about 10 miles of route, with three services to the south of the city (Oranjesig, Willows and Westdene) and a circular route via Aliwal Street to the Nordhoek in the north, returning to the city via Andries Pretorius Street or by an alternative route via Glen Street. There was also a short spur to the railway station. As with the two other early operators, single-deckers only were used initially, there being ten of these (Nos.1-10) built by the Railless Electric Construction Company Ltd, the builders of the system. These seated 25 and had rear platforms. This builder also supplied five single-deck trailers, seating 30, which were roofed but bereft of windows or doors. Unlike Germiston, which used the Cedes-Stoll system, Boksburg and Bloemfontein used conventional overhead. The system proved to be much more successful than either of the other pioneers, although it did not make a profit, and the "cars" suffered badly from the rough road surfaces of the period. In 1923 a visitor reported that they were noisy, their appearance was "deplorable" and that to ride in them was an ordeal. However, replacement vehicles had been ordered in 1922, and these consisted of three additional Railless (nos.11-13) and five Straker-Clough (probably nos.14-18) single-deckers. They were larger than the first generation trolleybuses and seated 34 and 38 respectively. They had rather curious open rear platforms, rather like contemporary Paris buses. Passengers no doubt appreciated the pneumatic tyres. Three further single-deckers, whose numbers have not been recorded, followed from Ransomes in 1927, these being 32-seaters of type D2. They had dual doorways and were fitted for one-man operation.

Finally in July 1930 a single Karrier-Clough E6 three-axle double-decker was delivered. This had BT-H electrical equipment with a 60hp motor and a double-deck body seating 33/28 built by Roe. Livery was green and cream. It was almost identical to a batch supplied by the same manufacturer to Doncaster Corporation and was tested on that system before leaving England. It was probably chassis

No.5 in Market Square in the early 1930s, with three of the 1922 single-deckers behind. The first of these appears to be pulling a trailer. (James Smith collection)

One of the Ransomes single-deckers. (Author's collection)

A builder's view of no.5. (John Whitehead collection)

number 54019, which is recorded as possibly having gone to Moçambique; it is quite likely that the vehicle was shipped to Bloemfontein through Lourenço Marques rather than by Cape Town. The trolleybus entered service as no.5 in August 1930 and was certainly the first double-deck trolleybus to run in normal service in South Africa, and probably the first to carry passengers. It was only the second double-decker of any kind to run in the country, the other being a Leyland Titan TD1 in Cape Town. However, no more trolleybuses of any kind were ordered and, as the system continued to lose money, it was subject to reports by both C. J. Spencer in 1934 (after he had reported on Johannesburg (qv)), and by Messrs L. M. Barry and W. Long, General Managers of Johannesburg and Cape Town respectively, in 1936. In both cases the recommendation was to replace the trolleybuses by motorbuses. The city was really too small to support the capital expenditure which was required for extensions and replacement of the 1922 vehicles. Double- and single-deck Leylands took over in October 1937 and further double-deckers of the same marque were bought after the second world war. None of the trolleybuses has survived.

Total number of double-deckers operated: 1

THE GUY DEMONSTRATOR

At almost the same time as no.5 was being placed in service in Bloemfontein, a double-deck Guy demonstration trolleybus was being unloaded at Cape Town docks. Under pressure from the members of the Kloof Civic Association, who were complaining vociferously about the tram service on the route to Tamboers Kloof, the board of City Tramways, a branch of Cape Electric Tramways, had accepted an offer

by Guy Motors Ltd to demonstrate a double-deck trolleybus in the city. The vehicle concerned was of three-axle design and probably had a Guy body; it was very similar to a batch supplied to Wolverhampton Corporation in 1931 and like these had a single step rear platform. It was 25ft 9in long and 7ft 4.5in wide and weighed nine tons. It arrived at Cape Town aboard *SS Halizones* on 29 August. F.J. Woodward, the representative of Guy Motors in South Africa, was anxious to see it running as soon as possible and it was first tried on the Rondebosch tram line, using a home-made trailing skate, made up from pieces of pipe threaded on to a chain, to provide for return current via one of the tram rails. The trolleybus was driven by P. Searle, foreman of the electrical department at Tollgate depot, and an assistant travelled on the rear platform to deal with the skate when, as happened frequently, it jumped out of the groove of the rail. Apparently he sustained several nasty shocks in the process. It was then run on the almost disused tram line to Wynberg, on which the overhead had been adapted to allow normal trolleybus

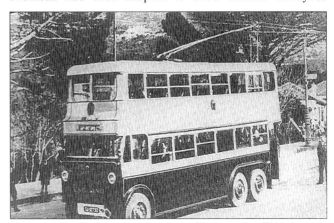

A view of the Guy in normal service, with two poles. This view was probably in Cape Town, in 1932. (Jimmy Madden collection)

operation, and it was there demonstrated on 10 September to both local councillors and a deputation from Johannesburg transport department. It was then demonstrated to another delegation, from Durban Corporation Tramways, and on 20 September it was run in public service to Tamboers Kloof. Such was the interest that the police had to be called in to control the crowd of would-be passengers and in fact it carried 85, rather more than its seating capacity of 59! All went well, however, and the public was enthusiastic.

It was then shipped to Durban for further demonstrations, at a cost of £200. It was driven via the tram route to Somerset Road, again using a skate, then run by gravity down a side street to the dock. Unfortunately it stopped 20 yards short of the ship and had to suffer the indignity of being pushed to the quayside. It arrived in Durban on 14 October and was tested on the Marine Parade tram route, using a skate for current return. From there the trolleybus was towed overland to Johannesburg in October and remained there until 16 November 1932, although not much used. It had to be registered to be able to run in that city and acquired the number TJ 12732. After a hair-raising journey of 1,500 miles on roads which were then little more than tracks and involving the fording of many rivers, it arrived safely back in Cape Town on 28 November. City Tramways had already received permission from the City Council, which was now very enthusiastic about trolleybuses, and from the Transportation Board, to erect a negative overhead wire in the anti-clockwise direction on the Gardens circle tram route, on which the track

was almost worn out. This was ready in March 1933 and the Guy was then hired by CT to operate for about a year on this line. It was then used as a pole carrier – the body having presumably been removed – during the conversion of the Wynberg and Sea Point trams, and was scrapped in 1939.

Although this pioneering venture certainly did much to convince South African operators of the benefits of the trolleybus, Guy Motors were not rewarded for their enterprise by any further orders from South Africa.

CAPE TOWN

Unlike the other systems in South Africa, that of Cape Town was run by a group of private companies under the general trading name of Cape Town Tramways. The local operation was generally referred to as "City Tramways". In the mid-1920s, following a depression in the gold mining industry, a finance group known as the Central Mining and Investment Corporation, decided to diversify into transport and, among other systems, invested in Cape Town Tramways. In 1925 it also obtained an interest in Weymann Motor Bodies Ltd., in Britain and, through its banking subsidiary of Bernard Scholle and Company Ltd., financed a considerable programme of expansion of that firm.

Cape Town had been a pioneer of electric tramway operation, service having begun in 1896. Both single- and double-deck vehicles were used. It was also in the forefront

Ransomes double-decker no.1 being unloaded at Cape Town. The South African Railways' tug *T.S. McEwen* is in attendance, but the event seems to have attracted only two spectators. (Museum of English Rural Life, University of Reading)

Ransomes no.3, unusually without any advertising material, at the Oranjezicht terminus of service 5 in Marmion Road. (Pam Eaton)

Traffic Ordinance. Agreement was not received until February 1934, and a draft ordinance to allow the replacement of trams was passed by the Provincial Council on 17 August 1934. The result was that Cape Town trolleybuses did not pay road tax and did not carry registration plates. A further impetus to the proposal had been given by the appointment in 1933 of A.C. Fenwick as Assistant General Manager; he had been rolling stock engineer at Dundee and had become enthusiastic about trolleybuses, based on his experience with these vehicles in Scotland. He later became General Manager.

In May a sales team from the firm of Ransomes, Sims and Jeffries of Ipswich arrived in Cape Town, having taken the novel step of flying out from Britain. They then provided a private film show for the CT board, using a 16mm film showing Ransomes trolleybuses in operation in New Zealand (Christchurch), and South America (Medellin), as well as in Britain. This film showed only single-deckers at work, but it must have been convincing, since it was decided to order 50 Ransomes trolleybuses, of which 30 would be double-deckers. All had the same chassis, but the suspension was strengthened on those chassis which were intended to carry double-deck bodywork. This was in fact the largest single order received by the manufacturer up to that time and was a definite coup for the small firm in face

of motorbus development, having begun its first service in 1911. By 1930 the condition of the older trams was beginning to cause concern.

Without waiting for the results of the second demonstration mentioned above, City Tramways in November 1932 applied to the City Council for permission to run what were in the city always referred to as "trackless trams". This usage even extended to advertisements on the sides of the trolleybuses, which exhorted the citizens of the city to "take this tram to Fletcher and Cartwright's Ltd. – Cape Town's best store"! The reason for the terminology was the financial advantage so gained, due to an oddity of the local Road

Ransomes no.17 negotiates a sharp bend and steep gradient, typical of the inland routes, inbound on service 2 at Tamboers Kloof. (Pam Eaton)

of competition from larger manufacturers – the advanced sales techniques had clearly paid off! Not surprisingly, in view of the financial link mentioned above, all the trolley-buses received Weymann metal-framed bodywork, this being the first export order for the firm. These bodies incorporated special insulation between the inner and outer panelling to keep the interior temperature down and also to prevent corrosion. In case of storms, a lightning conductor was provided on each bus and there were deep visors over the windows of each deck, to lessen the glare of the summer sun. The double-deckers were two-axle vehicles seating 62 or 64 passengers (sources differ) and numbered 1-30. One, number

Ransomes no.18 in an inner-suburban street, with some fine examples of colonial architecture on the right, overshadowed by more modern high-rise buildings behind. (Pam Eaton)

Single-deck Ransomes 32 and 39 with double-deckers 9 and 15 at Ebenezer Road sheds. (Pam Eaton)

En route to Sea Point on service 12 is no.84, one of the first batch of pre-war Sunbeams. (Pam Eaton)

unknown, was displayed on the MCW stand at the 1935 Commercial Motor Show in London before shipment. They were fitted with a Ransomes 2830 motor of 80hp, this being more powerful than that usually fitted by this manufacturer, to cope with the city's hills. Regenerative braking was fitted, with an estimated saving of 16% of the current used, with an air brake to bring the vehicle to a standstill. Lightweight Brecknell-Willis trolleys were fitted and originally an Indian bamboo pole was supplied to allow these to be turned manually when necessary. This was carried in a tube under the body. However, during the war, Indian bamboo became unavailable and a local product was substituted. Unfortunately these poles were too large to fit into the tube and a new tube had to be made for each vehicle; this protruded into the lower saloon and the seat backs on the left hand side had to be cut to accommodate it, while the end projected on to the platform. The single-deckers, nos.31-50, seated 39 passengers. Internally both classes were finished to a high standard, with comfortable seats upholstered in green leather, green rexine panelling and brown linoleum on the floor. Handrails were covered in white Doverite. However, unlike many contemporary buses these had lamps which were simply unshaded bulbs

The Ransomes, finished in grey primer, were shipped via the Port of London with interior fittings stowed inside the saloons for the voyage. Fleet livery was applied and the interior fittings put in place after arrival in Cape Town. The first arrived at Cape Town docks on 24 September 1935 and public service began with the line to Tamboers Kloof on 22 December. As more vehicles arrived, other tram services to Hanover Street, Warren Street, Oranjezicht, Kloof Street and Kloof Nek were converted and the Gardens circle now received a second set of overhead to allow trolleybuses to work in both directions. The Kloof Nek route was then the home of the single-deckers, due to its very steep gradients, but these also appeared on the Gardens service. To accommodate the fleet, a new depot was constructed at Ebenezer

Road, near Cape Town docks. In service these trolleybuses proved to be something of a disappointment and rapidly became unpopular with the running and maintenance staff. There were constant electrical problems, especially with the contactors, which were originally mounted on the chassis. Dirt and grit from the roads were easily able to lodge on them with sometimes frightening results, and they had to be removed to a position inside the cab. They were also particularly liable to dewirement, in which event the poles would shoot straight up into a vertical position, from which it was difficult to retrieve them. However, the chassis and bodywork were sound and the buses remained in service until 1962, though the single-deckers had gone at an earlier date. To cover a shortage of vehicles, eight of the double-deckers then underwent a conversion into singularly awkward-looking motorbuses, but this seems to have been successful and they ran as such for six years.

To allow conversion of the remaining tram services, to Wynberg and Sea Point, it was decided in 1937 to order 60 further double-deck trolleybuses and A.C. Fenwick, by now General Manager, and Rolling-stock Engineer L.R. Batchelor travelled, again by air, to see what was on offer at the Commercial Motor show held in London that autumn. The visitors were impressed by the chassis of the Sunbeam three axle MS2 on display, and placed an order for 60 of these. These had BT-H equipment, a 95hp motor and once again regenerative braking, as well as air brakes. A BT-H-Sims shaft generator provided current for a battery for lighting and to feed 60V traction batteries for manoeuvring. Given the experience with the Ransomes, the contactors were located in the cab from the beginning. In practice, the batteries proved to be incapable of moving even an empty trolleybus on anything but level ground, and they also occasionally disappeared while the trolleybus was standing at a terminus in one of the city's less salubrious suburbs. They were ultimately removed from the vehicles. Dimensions were 29ft 4¾in by 7ft 8in and fleet numbers 51-110. Again the all-metal bodies

10

A near-side view of no.91 on Service 12, but in an inner-suburban area. (Pam Eaton)

Sunbeam no.59 at Vredehoek on service 14. (Pam Eaton)

were supplied by Weymann and seated 66 passengers. Internally they were again well-finished, to the same standard as the Ransomes. For transport to South Africa, upper and lower decks were separated. When these had arrived in Cape Town and been reassembled, the Wynberg service was converted on 6 November 1938 and the last trams ran to Sea Point on the night of 28/29 January 1939. The former tram depot at Tollgate was rebuilt to house the Sunbeams.

A further ten almost-identical vehicles were ordered in 1939, and CT also decided to buy the Sunbeam demonstrator intended for the 1939 Commercial Motor Show, which was cancelled due to the outbreak of war. The only noticeable difference from the earlier batch was the lack of the Anshanco ventilator in the front roof dome. These buses, nos.111-121, went into service between November 1939 and January 1940 and on their arrival services to Devil's Peak, Vredehoek and Groote Schuur Hospital were converted from motorbus operation. The operator was certainly fortunate to receive the complete order before either U-boats or the British government could take their toll.

On 29 July 1943 the Company, supported by Cape Town Corporation and various other local authorities, applied to the Licensing Board for permission to convert the Bellville, Milnerton and Fresnaye motorbus services to trackless tram operation and, after due consideration, this was granted. As the war was drawing to a close, consideration was also given to extensions to Camp's Bay, as an extension of the Sea Point service, and to Bakoven. To work these, a further 25

Another view of some of the original fleet at home in Ebenezer Road depot in 1962. Single-decker no.32 is on the extreme left, with nos. 9 and 7 in the centre and no.16 on the right. (Pam Eaton)

Post-war Sunbeam no.140 bound for Sea Point on service 12 in 1962. (Pam Eaton)

Two Sunbeams outside Tollgate depot, the original tram sheds. (Pam Eaton)

Sunbeam MS2 vehicles were delivered in 1948, the first being bodied by Weymann in Britain and the remainder by Bus Bodies (SA) in Port Elizabeth. They were very similar to the pre-war buses but could be distinguished by their more angular appearance, rounded lower corners to the saloon windows and the absence of a green band below these. These took the numbers 122-146. Cost per vehicle had risen to £5,500. The Sunbeams proved to be reliable in service and were much appreciated by both passengers and maintenance staff. Unfortunately the plans for a service to Bellville foundered on the opposition of South African Railways, who already ran a frequent service of electric suburban trains to the area. The increase in the cost of overhead line and fittings probably also played a part in this decision and certainly put paid to the plans to run to Camp's Bay and Bakoven. This was a pity as it would have been one of the world's most scenic trolleybus routes. Plans for services to Milnerton and Fresnaye were quietly dropped. There was therefore a degree of over-capacity in the fleet, but as road improvements had in the meantime allowed double-deckers to run to Kloof Nek, some of the Sunbeams were placed on that service, at first on Sundays when heavy traffic was carried to connect with the cableway to the top of Table Mountain. Some of the single-deckers were then scrapped and others were converted into motorbuses for use by Boland Transport in the Stellenbosch area.

To provide adequate capacity on the service to Bellville, City Tramways in 1948 ordered 20 Daimler three-axle CVG6/6 motorbuses, with Weymann bodies similar to those of the trolleybuses. The chassis used was that of the Daimler CT type three-axle trolleybuses adapted to take a Gardner diesel engine. They were handsome and impressive machines but proved to be underpowered. When they were withdrawn in 1966, one was preserved through the efforts of John Grant-Silver and was driven by him, not without effort, to

Post-war Sunbeam no.136 on the turning circle at the terminus of the Kloof Nek route. (Pam Eaton)

No.17 in the city centre on 7 June 1957. (Noel Reed)

Johannesburg, where it can be seen in the James Hall Museum.

Unfortunately a change of control of the CT Company in 1956, when Tollgate Holdings – operators of the Golden Arrow motorbus services in the outer suburbs acquired a controlling interest – led to a decision, announced on 17 May 1962, to replace all trolleybuses as soon as possible. Conversion began with the Sea Point-Wynberg service later in 1962. The system was run down very quickly and by November 1963 the Tollgate sheds had been demolished to make way for a block of flats. Thereafter some vehicles had to be parked in the street overnight and, not surprisingly, some were vandalised. The last service, to Hanover Street, was converted to diesel bus operation on 28 February 1964, the last service bus being no.113, which made its final trip from Bree Street to Hanover Street around mid-day. Trolleybus 127 was decorated and illuminated for a tour of the route in the evening, additional equipment having been installed to cope with the increased lighting. It carried the Mayor, Mr Bill Peters, and was driven by J.P. Nel. One of the original drivers, Bill Muir, was also on board. No.127 was not scrapped at the time but set aside for preservation.

The livery of Cape Town trolleybuses was creamy-yellow with dark green bands around upper and lower deck windows, dark green mudguards and a silver roof. Many vehicles carried extensive advertising both in the normal position between decks and also below the lower saloon windows and on the rear platform and below the windscreen, but these had to conform to fairly strict guidelines set by the operator, which allowed the fleet livery to remain visible and only a single product was advertised on any one vehicle. The general appearance of the fleet was most attractive. Fortunately maintenance was to a high standard and the vehicles were immaculate right up to the end of service. Despite the introduction of apartheid after 1949, racial segregation was not practised on Cape Town's trolleybuses,

No.101 heading into the city centre on service 8 on 7 June 1957. (Noel Reed)

although, at least in the 1950s, service numbers were supplemented by the letters E and C, denoting that the destination was a "European" or a "Coloured" area respectively.

There were two AEC tower wagons, built in 1936 and 1938, and a Leyland Comet tower wagon acquired in 1949. In 1947 an ERF truck was obtained for general maintenance duties.

Ransomes 19 has been preserved in the James Hall Museum of Transport in Johannesburg but sadly Sunbeam 127 has not survived, having been allowed simply to rot away. Others were sold for use as garden huts, cricket pavilions and other roles, but none has lasted until the present time.

The trolleybuses served Cape Town well, operating every few minutes on the main routes and coping easily with the hills of the inland routes. It was a pity that they did not last until more value was placed on a quiet and pollution-free service.

Total number of double-deckers operated: 126

DURBAN

By 1930 Durban Corporation, which had taken over the privately-operated horse tramways in 1899 and electrified these in 1902/3, had built up a fleet of 120 double-deck trams. It had also begun to operate motorbuses in 1925, using single-deck vehicles only. Although a decision in principle to replace three tram services by trolleybuses had been taken in June 1930, Durban City Council seemed loath to give actual approval and no action was taken at the time. Impressed by the Guy demonstrator, the municipality, after some further deliberation, decided to replace the trams concerned by trolleybuses, and in November 1933 orders were placed for 22 two-axle double-deckers, these being equally divided between Sunbeam (MF2) and Leyland (TBD2). The former had BT-H equipment and the latter GEC. Fleet numbers were 1-11 and 12-22. Bodywork was by Park Royal, seating 55. The buses had a slightly dated appearance, having short bonnets and heavy trolley gantries. Each complete bus cost £4,000. The first arrived at the docks on 27 August 1934 on board *SS Umkuzi* and on 30 January 1935 no.1 made a trial run with civic dignitaries on the Marine Parade service. The formal opening of the first service by the Mayor, Mr Fleming-Johnson took place on Saturday 23 February, when all 22 vehicles were lined up on the north side of West Street, between Church Street and Aliwal Street, facing east, in numerical order. Invited guests were then taken on a tour of the system in the trolleybuses, starting from the main police station in West Street at 2.30pm. Public service began on the following day, with services to The Point and to Marine Parade.

As the trolleybuses made a profit of £9,324 in their first twenty-nine months of operation, the conversion was deemed to be a success and plans were then made to replace all the remaining trams. In August 1937 tenders were invited for 25 three-axle double-deck trolleybuses and orders were subsequently placed for these, being once again split between two manufacturers. They were for 12 Sunbeam MS2s with BT-H equipment and 13 AEC 664Ts. The Sunbeams had Metro-Cammell bodywork seating 71 passengers and the AECs had English Electric bodies, seating 70. The first eight Sunbeams, nos.23-30, and all the AECs, nos.31-43, arrived in 1939 and the remaining four Sunbeams, nos.44-47, in 1940. Prior to their arrival, trolleybus services were inaugurated to South

The trolleybuses were still a novelty in 1936, when some running repairs to Sunbeam no.7 on West Street at Marine Parade attracted several interested spectators. (Kevan J. Mardon collection)

A line of trolleybuses and some vintage motor cars in West Street on 15 February 1962. From right to left the vehicles are 224, 202, 2052, 2066, unknown and 2048. (Kevan J. Mardon collection)

Sunbeam no.5 when new in West Street. (Kevan J. Mardon collection)

Trolleybuses are generally a very safe form of transport, but on 5 March 1941 Leyland no.15 came to grief on West Street at a point where a railway line crossed it, near the intersection of Kearnsey Road and Farewell Street. The railway track caused a distinct bump in the road surface and it is thought that the driver, not wanting to jolt his passengers on this, over-compensated on the steering, causing the trolleybus to skid on the railway tracks. Thirty-seven passengers were injured, but no.15 was little damaged and was soon hauled upright again with the aid of a steam crane. It is claimed that this is the only recorded case anywhere of overturning by a double-deck trolleybus. (Kevan J. Mardon collection)

Beach on 26 February 1938 and to Kingsmead on 3 October. Later in 1937 a further order was placed for 42 Leyland TTB5 vehicles with Metro-Cammell bodywork. Of these 29 were to have GEC equipment and 13 were to have Metropolitan-Vickers equipment. The outbreak of war did not immediately interfere with the tramway replacement process and new buses continued to arrive into 1941, to allow the conversions to continue. These were numbered 48-62 and 64/5; the trolleybus which should have become no.63 became London Transport no.1725, but for some reason Durban failed to correct their numbering scheme to take account of this. Using these vehicles, the tram service to Umbilo, with its branch

On the opening of the service in February 1935, nos.14 and 5 demonstrate their flexibility as they overtake bogie tram no.93 on Point Road. (Kevan J. Mardon collection)

The only reversing triangle in Durban was on Point Road at Browns Road, being negotiated by no.6 in 1936. Durban was the only system to make provision for the carriage of deep sea fishing rods on its trolleybuses and several can be seen stowed on the back of no.6. (Kevan J. Mardon collection)

to Stellawood Cemetery, was converted in July 1939, with a new turning loop at the terminus which took the trolleybuses well beyond the former tram terminus in Bartle Road. A new branch was constructed to Penzance Road, not previously served by trams. Conversion of the Tollgate service, with an extension to the foot of Mayville Hill, followed in December 1940. In February 1941 the Glenwood service was converted, to be followed one month later by that to Overport. There was also a new direct route, not previously served by trams, from Berea Road via Alice Street to the sea front at the pavilion. Unfortunately this failed to attract much traffic and was

withdrawn in 1943 as a war-time economy measure. It was not re-opened after the war. The trolleybuses continued to be profitable and in the year 1939-40 made a profit of £12,925.

By late 1941 the dangers to shipping posed by U-boats and the needs of London allowed the British government to commandeer the 25 vehicles of this order which had not then set out for Africa. The first was handed over to London's LPTB in November 1941 and the others between February and August 1942. To allow the operation of buses which were eight feet wide, special dispensation had to be given by the Metropolitan Police. These trolleybuses were put to work from Ilford depot, the front exit doorways being sealed off and a longitudinal seat for two being placed across it. About half of the full-drop opening windows were sealed shut, but the darkened "purdah" glass in the upper portions of the windows remained until the end, except on the few cases where breakages had to be replaced. In London they seated 72 passengers. They included all those with M-V equipment, which became class SA2, nos.1734-1746, and 12 with GEC equipment, which became class SA1, nos.1722-1733. All ran successfully in London until 1959. In Durban, the conversion scheme had perforce to come to a halt and the system's 28 bogie trams had to continue to maintain some services. In fact, the Musgrave Road service, which had been part-converted to diesel buses in 1940, reverted to full-time tramway operation in August 1943.

When it seemed that the end of the war was in sight, the municipality ordered 52 three axle MS2 vehicles from

AEC no.43 on Ridge Road in 1948. (Kevan J. Mardon collection)

On a driver training run in 1940, AEC no.33 passes bogie trams nos.103 and 100 on Umbilo Road at Queen Mary Avenue. (Kevan J. Mardon collection)

Sunbeam in July 1945, but owing to shortages these did not enter service in Durban until 1948/9. They were to have been 66-117 but by this time the former system of fleet numbers had been changed to one which would coincide with the registration numbers and the new trolleybuses were therefore 2023-2074. One was displayed with its intended number 90 at the first post-war motor show at Earl's Court in 1947. These were on MS2 chassis, with BT-H electrical equipment. The first 27 to arrive came complete with Metro-Cammell bodies, seating 72, the next 20 were bodied in South Africa by Bus Bodies (SA) Ltd and the final five were bodied by BMS, British Mining Supplies Ltd. These last had a much more rounded design of coachwork. With the arrival of these trolley-buses, the conversion scheme was resumed and the last trams ran to Umgeni and North Ridge Road early in 1948, this latter service being extended to meet the Overport service and create a circular route. The short spur to the racecourse was also converted to trolleybus operation. The Musgrave Road was re-converted to motorbuses in August 1949, bringing tramway operation in Durban to an end. This route was finally converted to trolleybus operation on 1 May 1960, using vehicles which had previously served the Umgeni and Mayville Hill routes, these being converted to motorbuses. There were short extensions to the trolleybus network in Berea in 1950, at Marine Parade in 1959 and to South Beach in 1961.

The remainder of the fleet was in 1947 renumbered by manufacture as follows:

1-11	2000-2010
12-22	2200-2210
23-30	2011-2018
31-43	2400-2412
44-47	2019-2022
48-62	2211-2227
and 64/5	

Originally the fleet number served also as the registration number but registration plates with the prefix NDC (Natal Durban Corporation) were introduced in 1955.

A near side view of no.2067 seen passing the Royal Hotel in Smith Street at Church Street. This trolleybus was displayed on the Sunbeam stand at the first post-war Commercial Motor Show, held in London in 1947. (Kevan J. Mardon collection)

No.2073 (BMS body) with rebodied Daimler motorbus no.3009 at the war memorial in Church Street in 1962. (Kevan J. Mardon collection)

A fine view of no.2041 in 1953, showing the majestic lines of the post-war Sunbeams. (John Allen, courtesy Kevan J. Mardon)

Features common to all Durban trolleybuses were the provision of a forward exit with an air-operated sliding door and the fitting of dark "purdah" glass in the upper portions of all windows, as a protection against the glare of the Natal sun.

The arrival of the last Sunbeams allowed the transport department to transfer the 22 two-axle vehicles to the "Non-European" Market – The Point service, but they did not last long on these, as the service was abandoned in 1950 and the vehicles scrapped. In 1955 the AEC class were also withdrawn, owing to structural defects in the bodywork. One became a single-deck toastrack motorbus for use on the services along the sea front, in which capacity it lasted until about 1960.

No further new vehicles were bought and the trolleybuses began to experience a very lingering death. The Kingsmead and Racecourse services went over to motorbus operation in 1962, followed by Penzance Road in 1963. The next year saw the end of services to Umbilo, Glenwood, and The Point on 2 August and after that date trolleybuses operated during mornings only. The last of the 1939/40 Sunbeams and the last Leylands in service ran in May 1967. The Berea area services finished on 31 July 1967, leaving only those to South Beach and Marine Parade. The final service run was made on the Marine Parade route on the morning of 11 April 1968 by Sunbeam 2040 and when it returned to the depot at 09.00, the era of public service by trolleybus in Durban came to an end.

However, Leyland 2222 had been purchased for preservation thanks to the efforts of John Grant-Silver and James Hall, founder of the transport museum which bears his name in Johannesburg. It was restored to almost original condition by the workshop staff, who were able to refit the bus with many fittings long since removed or replaced. On 1 March 1968, its original number of 59 restored, it was used for an official farewell tour, carrying the Mayor, Mrs. Margaret Maytom, councillors and municipal officials. This tour took it from the City Hall to the Marine Parade terminus and back again, and those on board commented favourably on the smooth and quiet ride. It was driven by Arthur Reeve who had taken it out on its first run in 1941. In the afternoon of the same day, it left its native city for Johannesburg, where on arrival it made a tour of the system before retiring to the James Hall Museum of Transport for preservation.

The original livery of Durban Corporation trolleybuses was grey with cream bands and it is in this condition that no.59 has been preserved. From 1953 onwards, this was changed to red and off-white with silver roof. However, in later years many vehicles were almost totally covered with advertisements. Trolleybuses used on what were termed "unreserved" services (i.e., those for African passengers) were originally painted green and later designated by a green band below the lower deck windows. From October 1953 the upper decks on all double-deck vehicles were designated "unreserved" and were thus open to all races, though all passengers were charged "European" fares, which were generally about 33% more than the "Non-European" fares.

To increase ventilation in the upper saloon, it was quite common for trolleybuses to run in service with the rear window lowered to the horizontal position.

Apart from the original two-axle vehicles, all trolleybuses were fitted with run-back and coasting brakes, to allow their use on the hilly routes in the Berea area. In later years many trolleybuses were substantially rebuilt and then had front upper deck windows and destination boxes mounted in rubber pans, a change which did nothing for their appearance, and in the last years, the previously-smart fleet assumed a run-down appearance. In December 1964, Sunbeam 2067 was illuminated and toured the streets for the month before Christmas. A

A lively scene in West Street in 1958 with large US cars, trolleybuses and a rickshaw jostling for road space – but, the original caption points out, all had to obey the robots (traffic lights). (Kevan J. Mardon collection)

It was uncommon latterly to find a Durban trolleybus in fleet livery, but 2064, one of the post-war vehicles, displays the final version of this to advantage. The trolleybus is leaving Marine Parade terminus for Umbilo. (Roger M. Perry)

loudspeaker system was fitted to play suitably festive music and the enterprise proved to be popular with the public. However, it was not repeated in any later year.

The Durban trolleybuses were popular and served the city well. However, from about 1955 the transport department had begun to change its entire system to single-deck operation, probably as the best method of coping with the economic consequences of apartheid, and the double-deckers, both electric and diesel, were on the way out. No consideration seems to have been given to the purchase of single-deck trolleybuses.

Total number of double-deckers operated: 116

By contrast, another of the same batch displays an all-over advertising livery at Marine Parade terminus, September 1967. (Roger M Perry)

Nos.18 and 24 in the depot when new. (Les Pivnic collection)

JOHANNESBURG

This municipality had begun to operate electric trams in 1906, having previously taken over the company which provided horse tram services. After a brief experiment in 1913/4, motorbus services were begun on a permanent basis in 1927. Although the Guy demonstrator mentioned elsewhere visited this city in 1930, the transport department of the Johannesburg municipality was not convinced of its usefulness as a replacement for its tramways and nothing came of the demonstration. However, in 1934 a special commission, known from its chairman – C.J. Spencer

This vehicle, despite appearances, is not a double-deck trolleybus, but a former motorbus which has been adapted to grease the trolleybus overhead. (James Smith collection)

No.38, the last of the second batch of Sunbeams, is seen at the junction of the Rosebank and Dunkeld routes, while on the right workmen prepare to give the overhead some attention from a vintage tower wagon. (J.V. Horn, author's collection)

formerly of the Metropolitan Electric Tramways in London – as the Spencer commission, was appointed to review the future of the city's transport, and in its report this body recommended the use of trolleybuses on certain routes. Unusually, the routes chosen, those running along Louis Botha Avenue in the north east part of the city, were not at that time operated by trams but by diesel buses, which had replaced trams some years earlier. Due to the city's altitude of 5,500ft and the hilly nature of the routes concerned, bus operation had not been totally successful or popular and it was suggested that trolleybuses would be a more suitable form of transport in the northern part of the city. There was no suggestion that trolleybuses should be used to replace the entire tram system in the immediate future and indeed the city had just taken delivery of 50 modern streamlined bogie cars.

The proposal was adopted by the City Council and orders were placed for 22 double-deck trolleybuses. Half were on AEC 661T chassis with English Electric equipment, nos.12-22, and half on Sunbeam MF2 chassis with British Thomson-Houston regenerative equipment, nos.1-11. In both cases 80hp motors were fitted. Total cost was £72,000. All were given bodywork by Metro-Cammell, seating 60 passengers, with standing room for (officially) 12. For use by lower saloon passengers at city termini, front exits were fitted. Unlike contemporary buses in Britain, these were 8 feet wide. Internally there were red rexine panels and red leather seats and the interior lights were in recessed fittings, covered with frosted glass. The upper half of the windows had darkened "purdah" glass and roller blinds could be lowered to keep out the glare of the sun. These were indeed luxurious vehicles for city service and with them service was begun to Sydenham on 26 August 1936. Two branch extensions, to Norwood and, in 1938, to Highlands North, followed and on 4 April 1938 the bus service to Rosebank and Dunkeld, in the north of the city, was converted to trolleybus operation and a branch to Parktown North was added along Seventh Avenue and Tyrwhitt Road, from which the tram service had been withdrawn in 1935. Eight additional buses of each type were delivered for this route, nos.23-30 being by AEC and 31-38 by Sunbeam. These were similar to the first batch, but had rather thicker window pillars and the interior lights were placed in Art Deco "jelly mould" shades. The last of the Sunbeams, no.38, was finished to an even higher standard and was shown at the Earls Court motor show in November 1937. All these trolleybuses had regenerative brakes, but this feature gave problems in the substations if too many vehicles regenerated at the same time, and the feature was not repeated on post-war deliveries. All these buses were renumbered 501-538 in the late 1940s and all were withdrawn

One of the original vehicles at Parktown North in pre-war days. (Les Pivnic collection)

between 1955 and 1960. In the year 1939-40, the trolleybuses made a small loss of just over £1,000.

On 5 May 1939 the city council adopted plans to convert the tram services to Melville and Parktown North and the motorbus service to Westdene to trolleybus operation. It was planned to use both two- and three-axle double-deckers and 55 vehicles were ordered on 22 August 1939. There would have been 30 three-axle AEC 664T vehicles and 25 two-axle Sunbeams, all with M-C bodies. The original tender accepted for the six-wheelers was in fact from Leyland, but for some reason this was cancelled and a tender from AEC was accepted in

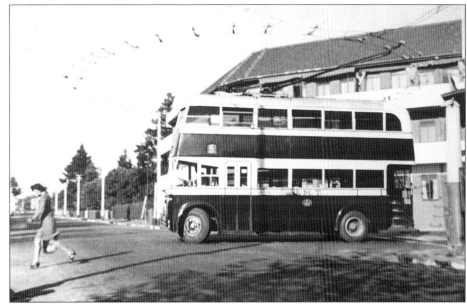

A nearside view of a pre-war trolleybus turning at Parktown North. (J.V. Horn, author's collection)

The junction of Dunottar Street and Louis Botha Avenue. On the right Sunbeam no.32 is turning off the latter en route to Sydenham on service 14, while on the left no.25 heads for the city. (J. V. Horn, author's collection)

No.21 on service 5 shares Parktown North terminus with tram no.221 on service L1 in 1945. (B. T. Cooke, author's collection)

In 1962 no.572 awaits departure from Dunkeld terminus on "Non European" service, while one of the large Sunbeams or Alfa-Romeos passes on the left. (Pam Eaton)

its place. However, as far as Johannesburg was concerned, the matter became academic, since in 1941 the 18 completed AEC buses were diverted by the British government to London Transport and placed in service in the Ilford area as class SA3 nos.1747-1764. They were modified in a similar manner to the Durban vehicles and the offside number box peculiar to Johannesburg was not used. In London they

seated 72 passengers and they went into service between June 1942 and June 1943, lasting until 1959. The remainder of this order was not built. The chassis for the Sunbeams had been completed but they were at this stage still awaiting bodywork. They were likewise taken over and fitted with austerity bodywork in 1942, these being the only such bodies to be 8ft wide. They were then allocated to Nottingham (5)

No.597 in original condition climbing to the leafy suburb of Greenside on service 77 in 1962. (Pam Eaton)

A service was provided to the exhibition grounds in Milner Park at times of special events and in 1962 no.577 is turning off Showground Road on to the loop which served the site. All buses on special services, to any destination, displayed the number 98, which could be seen in different parts of the city. (Pam Eaton)

and Bradford (10), These had Weymann bodywork. The balance of ten went to St. Helens, these being given Massey lowbridge bodywork. In Johannesburg the trams to the north west suburbs soldiered on.

After the end of the war, an order was placed to replace the trolleybuses which had been diverted to London. At the same time, a further order was placed for 30 additional AEC three-axle vehicles, making a total of 60 new three-axle trolley-buses. Following the merging of trolleybus production of AEC and Leyland as British United Traction in 1946, these were of course built as BUT 9641T. These were to replace the two tram services. The order for the 25 two-axle Sunbeam W trolleybuses was also re-confirmed. The BUTs, later known as "first series", had electrical equipment by English Electric, with 125hp motors. The first, no.564, was completed by Metro-Cammell and, in workshop grey, was tested in 1948 under London Transport wiring in the Hampton Court area before being shipped off to South Africa. Bodywork for 44 others, nos.565-608, was shipped in sections and mounted locally by Bus Bodies (SA) Ltd. The remainder, nos.609-623, had bodies by British Mining Supplies Ltd (BMS), built in South Africa, but with a distinct flavour of contemporary Park Royal designs, as BMS was a subsidiary of that firm. All had, in addition to the normal open rear platform and stairs, front exits, a seating capacity of 71 and an official standing capacity of 13. These were placed in service on the routes to Melville in June 1948 and to Parktown North in October of the same year, this being the first occasion on which trolley-buses directly replaced trams in Johannesburg. The former service also replaced the Westdene motorbus service, while the latter was extended to Parkhurst. In August of the same year, they were also used to replace motorbuses on the services to Greenside and a spur was later constructed from this route to Parkview. From the point where the Melville

A close-up of the "points boy" operating the frog at the same location. (Pam Eaton)

No.606 inbound on Louis Botha Avenue, working from Highlands North on service 13 in 1962. (Pam Eaton)

First series BUT no.606 awaiting departure for Forest Hill from van der Byl Square, terminus for all services to the southern suburbs. (Roger M. Perry)

No.620 with its original body is outward bound for Melville in Jorissen Street, Braamfontein, passing some typical inner suburban housing and the Albert cinema on the right. Workmen are putting finishing touches to the road surface after removal of the tram tracks. The overhead wires coming in from the left are from Jan Smuts Avenue and the inbound trolleybus is on what was then service 9 from Parkhurst. It was later renumbered 79. (Les Pivnic collection)

The lower saloon of no.580 mounted on a rail flat wagon for transport from the builders in Port Elizabeth to Johannesburg. (James Smith collection)

route left Kingsway at Lothbury Road, a branch was later constructed to Auckland Park and extended to Triomf.

In 1960 eight of the BMS-bodied vehicles (616-623), which were found to be suffering from structural weakness, were either rebodied or very substantially rebuilt by J. Brockhouse and Co., as successors to BMS, with an increased seating capacity of 73. In 1962 or 1963 nos.611-615 were similarly treated, leaving only nos.609 and 610 of this class in their original state. Of these, the upper deck of the former was either substantially rebuilt or renewed completely. No.610 alone retained its original appearance until withdrawal. In later years, these vehicles were used only on what were known as the "Non-European" services (2, 77 and 79A), these being also identified by a green board above the windscreen with the wording "Non-Whites Only – Slegs Nie-Blankes".

Six others (577, 579, 587, 588, 593 and 601) were in 1969

No.620, as rebodied, in the city centre in September 1977. (Author)

No.611 with BMS body at the suburban terminus of service 44 at South Hills in 1971. (W.D. Howarth, author's collection)

No.593 after conversion for OMO, on Kingsway outward bound to Triomf (W.D. Howarth, author's collection)

No.588 as converted for OMO leaves the city for Berea on a short working of service 20, September 1977. (Author)

The central trolleybus depot in Fordsburg. (W.D. Howarth, author's collection)

BUT no.579, leaving the city centre for Berea in August 1977, shows clearly that it has been given a new front staircase in its conversion for OMO. (Author)

converted for one-man operation. This involved the fitting of an additional staircase at the front and, in some cases, such as no.593, replacement of the existing front exit by a rather strange design of sliding door mounted on the outside of the body. In other conversions, such as no.579, conventional folding doors were retained at the front. All received conventional folding doors to the rear platform. As these conversions proved successful, others were similarly treated at a later date. Some of this class also received considerable body rebuilds, being given rubber-mounted windows with hopper ventilators and others had horizontally-sliding windows fitted, but others remained in original condition until withdrawal, by which time scarcely any one bus looked quite like any other. Withdrawal of this class was a gradual process,

Post-war Sunbeam no.539 on service 79A to Parktown North, in Harrison Street about 1960. (Tony Spit, author's collection)

being spread throughout the 1970s, and many latterly spent a considerable time in store. The last two in service were nos.1593 and 1601 which were withdrawn in 1978, re-commissioned in 1979 and finally retired on 23 April 1981. The first series of BUTs had indeed given excellent service.

Post-war Sunbeam no.553 approaching Melville terminus on service 67. (Pam Eaton)

No.659, in original condition, in de Villiers Street near the railway station, in September 1977. It is working on service 2 to Dunkeld. (Author)

BUT no.638, seen in the city centre in 1977, has been rebuilt for OMO, but still retains its rear platform. (Author)

No 652 as converted for one person operation at Homestead Park terminus in September 1977. (Author)

At Townsview, in the southern suburbs, service 47 buses turned by reversing into Prairie Street then out again into Valda Street in a rather complex manoeuvre, which here seems to demand the services of an inspector to control other traffic. The trolleybus is no.612. (W.D. Howarth, author's collection)

Services for black African passengers started from a separate bus station located in Frazer Street, between Jeppe and Bree Streets. In August 1977 two BUTs await departure on service 79A to Parktown North, while the driver of an AEC Regent V motorbus on service 2A to Dunkeld has time for a chat. (Author)

The Sunbeams, nos. 539-563, were bodied by Bus Bodies, seating 60 passengers, and were delivered in 1948. They had BT-H 100hp motors but proved to be too small to deal adequately with Johannesburg's heavy peak hour traffic and all had been withdrawn by 1970.

In 1949 all earlier trolleybuses were renumbered in sequence from 501 upwards.

The need to replace the first generation of trolleybuses and the decision to convert most of the remainder of the tramways to trolleybus operation led to the placing of further orders in 1957. Additionally, it was decided to convert to trolleybus operation services in the southern suburbs on which motorbuses had replaced trams in the 1930s. Fifty three-axle BUT 9642T vehicles, nos.624-673, arrived in 1958. These were often referred to as "second series BUTs" and had Bus Bodies bodywork, seating 73 passengers with standing room for 12. English Electric electrical equipment was fitted. Using some of these, the Mayfair tram service was converted to trolleybus operation on 30 March 1958, being extended by half a mile to Homestead Park. In mid-1960 the motorbuses which had replaced the tram services to Yeoville and Observatory on 30 January were replaced by trolleybuses, the latter service being extended to Bellevue. The services to the southern suburbs, which had been converted from trams to diesel buses in 1935, were now also converted to trolleybuses and a new depot was opened at Trojan to house these. These covered the services running south via Eloff Street extension, which branched at Trojan depot to serve five separate termini. These conversions brought the system to its peak of 15 "European" and three "Non European" services, worked by a fleet of 175 vehicles. All other tram services were replaced by diesel buses.

In 1968 nos.624-648 were converted for one-man operation and then had a capacity of 69+19. In this case the rear platform was simply enclosed and the stairs remained in their former position there, the former front exit being used for both entry and exit. The conversions were successful and showed that it was possible to operate double-deckers of traditional layout by one person. Nos. 649-653 underwent a more thorough rebuilding, the stairs being moved to the front, the rear platform removed and replaced by additional seating space and the former front exit being used for entry and exit. The rest of the class, with the exception of no.663, were converted between 1976 and 1979, when five stored vehicles were also returned to traffic. These later conversions, which followed the layout of 624-648, were used on the "Non-European" services to Dunkeld and Parktown North. All services became one-man operated from 1 August 1980. Some of this class received very heavy overhauls, almost amounting to rebuildings, at this time.

Finally there arrived in Johannesburg the largest double-deck trolleybuses ever built. In 1956 an order was placed for 40 Sunbeam S7A chassis, but it seems that Sunbeam were experiencing some difficulty with this order and in the event 20 were constructed in Italy by Alfa-Romeo, the only double-deck trolleybuses built by this firm. The buses which would have formed the balance of the order were completed as

Alfa-Romeo no.675 en route to Townsview in the southern suburbs. (Tony Spit, author's collection)

Guy three-axle motorbuses, with Rolls-Royce engines. Trolleybuses and buses alike had bodies by Bus Bodies and they were 35ft. 6in. long and seated 85 passengers, with space for 22 standees. The Sunbeams were numbered 694-713 and had BT-H equipment with 160hp motors, while the Alfa-Romeos, nos.674-693, had Ansaldo equipment with 152hp motors. Despite their great size, they were successful and coped well with heavy peak-hour loadings. On 9 October 1967 a fire, of unknown origin, at Trojan depot destroyed nos. 699, 701, 704 and 709, as well as BUT no.677 and these were not repaired. The Alfa-Romeos generally operated only on the services to the southern suburbs until these were withdrawn on 30 June 1973. Thereafter a few appeared on peak hour workings to Bera and Bellevue, services 20B and 20A, and others were transferred to "Non European" services. However, as they had proved to be prone to mechanical and electrical failure, all were withdrawn between 1972 and 1974. Of the Sunbeams, nos.702 and 706 were withdrawn in 1976 and nos.1695 and 1710 were withdrawn in 1981, but the remainder survived until the end, having been converted to one-person operation during the first half of 1980.

All surviving trolleybuses had 1000 added to their fleet numbers in 1978.

Johannesburg then went on to become the only British-type system to place in service a third generation of double-deck trolleybuses. By 1980 South Africa was feeling the pressure of sanctions and the government was interested in the possibilities of developing electric street transport. Acting in co-operation with the city council, the National Transport Commission decided in March 1980 to experiment with new vehicles on a service from Twist Street through the city centre to Forest Hill. This was a combination of two previous routes, on which the overhead was still in place, and it was

No.672, still in original condition, leaves the city terminus in Frazer Street at Bree Street in September 1977. (Author)

the only trolleybus service ever operated which did not terminate in the centre. The NTC met 60% of the costs of the experiment, the balance being met by Johannesburg City Council. A very new British firm, Quest 80 Ltd (founded in 1979), were employed as consultants with the local Sigma Power Corporation Ltd, to develop plans for a new generation of trolleybuses and in the event went on to build one of the prototypes themselves, on a Metrobus chassis. Orders for the trolleybuses were placed in May 1980 and details of the double-deckers were as follows:

Experimental trolleybus no.800 at Hillbrow. (Jimmy Madden, James Smith collection)

A rear view of no.801 (left) with no.803, on the Auckland Park service. (John Fran, courtesy Kevan J. Mardon)

800   Mercedes-Benz. Busaf. BBC/Sècheron, chopper control, 155kW motor, 94 seats, no standees, final cost (complete) R178,780 (c.£35,756)

801   Sigma E1/Quest. Busaf BBC/TCO, 160kW motor, 84 seats, no standees. Final cost (complete) R189,298 (c.£37,859). This vehicle was built on a chassis of an MCW Metrobus and is (at present) the last trolleybus to be built in Britain for export. That firm had in 1979/80 completed an order for 40 Metrobus DR105/1 motor buses of 11.45m length for China Motor Bus of Hong Kong and a further chassis was constructed for the Johannesburg trolleybus.

802   Springfield, Ansaldo, "Era" electronic control, 110kW motor, 89 seats, 11 standees. Final cost R141,511 plus body, probably c.R178,000

803   Springfield, Toshiba chopper control. Final cost R155,776

804   Springfield, AEG, chopper control. No information on capacity. Final cost R185,166. It is not clear if this included the cost of the body. If it did not, this was a very expensive bus indeed!

(Springfield Diesel (Pty) Ltd is a South African firm based in Isando)

Single-decker no.805 seen in the former no.2 tram shed. (Jimmy Madden, James Smith collection)

Single-decker no.806 on a low loader. (John Fran, courtesy Kevan J. Mardon)

The two articulated single-deckers, nos.805/6, proved to be more expensive, costing R185,652 and R188,944 complete. These were both built by Springfield, with equipment by GEC (no.805) (chopper) and Siemens (no.806). It was perhaps rather optimistic to include articulated single-deckers in the demonstration fleet, since the Johannesburg travelling public had decisively rejected the concept when an articulated single-deck motorbus was tried for four months in the first half of 1980.

At that time, a double-deck motorbus of the type being supplied to Johannesburg – Mercedes-Benz with Busaf body, would have cost about R80,000.

All of the new fleet had auxiliary motors to be used in depot areas and avoid the need for complex overhead wiring. The single-deckers and no.800 had VW petrol engines, the others, except for no.802, Magirus-Deutz diesels. No.802 had a Hattz diesel. All bodies looked similar and were very similar to those then being fitted to double-deck motorbuses for the city. The first to run was no.800, which went out to Parktown North on 30 June 1981. It was displayed on the stand of Messrs Dorbyl, the parent company of Busaf, at an international transport exhibition in Johannesburg from 27 July to 1 August and then entered revenue service, but problems with differentials soon had it confined to the depot and it did not run normally until November, by which date a replacement part had been sent from Germany. It then ran on the Melville and Parkhurst services, but was again off the road in March/April 1982 apparently due to problems with the power steering. Originally painted in JTD fleet livery of dark red and ivory, this bus was soon repainted into the NTC colours of blue, orange and white. Not unreasonably, that body wished the public to be aware of its involvement with a project into which it had put a considerable sum of money, R1.5m. or approximately £300,000 at the then rate of exchange. No.801, in a white livery, followed soon after, but suffered a bent rear axle before entering service and had to be returned to the builders for repair. There were then problems with the electrical equipment and this bus did not enter service until January 1982. After a delay awaiting a new 24-volt unit, which had to be sent out from England, it ran fairly consistently on normal service until the beginning of the demonstration project in August. No.802 was handed over in September 1981, also in NTC colours, but problems with its air bag suspension prevented it entering service until March 1982, when, on Sunday 20, it made one sortie into public service. This ended in a minor disaster, when it managed to bring down a section of overhead near Milner Park. Then on 26 April Sunbeam no.1712 ran into it in the depot, causing considerable damage to the rear end, necessitating extensive repairs to the body and auxiliary equipment. (The same Sunbeam had previously caused a Foden tower wagon to meet a premature end, by pushing it into a traction pole.) No.803 arrived in January 1982 but, despite an enthusiastic reception by drivers, proved to have so many faults that it had to be returned to the builders in February, from where it returned at the end of April. The last double-decker followed in the summer of 1982.

As commissioning was thus prolonged, the start of revenue service on the demonstration route was first put back to April 1982 and in the event did not begin until 4 August 1982. On that date an opening ceremony was held, in

No.803 negotiating the tight corner from Nugget Street into Twist Street in Hillbrow, while working on the demonstration service. (John Fran, courtesy Kevan J. Mardon)

perfect weather, in the members' car park at Turffontein race course, which all vehicles except no.805 (which was on a low loader) reached under their own power using the wires of the Forest Hill route to Turffontein Road, whence they proceeded by means of the auxiliary diesel motors. Unfortunately no.803 didn't quite make it and had to be rescued by jumper cables. In a ribbon-bedecked pavilion in the centre of the exhibition area various bus body manufacturers displayed their wares, while outside, on tables shaded by parasols, the various manufacturers who had supplied equipment for the new trolleybuses each had a stand. Two of the old fleet were also on display, nos.1630 and 1694, a banner across their cabs proclaiming "Trolleybuses of Yesteryear". Despite this ageist comment, both vehicles were back in public service on the following day! After a brief speech in which he mentioned the need to tackle congestion, and suggested that by the year 2000 one million vehicles could be entering the central area of Johannesburg each day, the Minister of Transport Affairs, the Hon. Hendrik Schoeman, cut a tape to inaugurate the service and guests boarded the new vehicles for a tour to Hillbrow and return, champagne being served en route. The order of the procession was single-decker 805, followed by double-deckers 800, 801, 804, 802 and 803, in that order. At Hillbrow the participants changed vehicles, to allow them to sample several and while they were doing so, were entertained by the Witwatersrand Command Band. The procession then returned to Turffontein for pre-lunch drinks on the terrace at the race course. The Mayor of Johannesburg, Danie van Zyl, then welcomed guests to lunch. It must indeed have been a proud day for him, since as an opposition member of the city council he had, in 1973, strongly argued for the retention of the trolleybus system, against the views of the-then majority United Party. The proceedings were brought to a close after lunch by an address from the Director General: Transport, Mr A.B. Eksteen. An enthusiasts' tour was held on the following Saturday, 7 August, using no.800 and no.1630 of the old fleet.

It seemed an auspicious beginning for the new service, but matters did not go according to plan. Of the individual vehicles, the Mercedes no.800 had some problems with the trolley retrievers, which tended to pull the booms off the wires. Despite this, it appears to have been the best performer, since it achieved a total of 41,744km in service by July 1985. As the total mileage run during the entire project (from August 1981) was 131,373km, this one bus accounted for almost one third of the total, although it was off the road from November 1984 to April 1985, after the roof and the equipment mounted thereon had been damaged when it was towed under a low bridge in Braamfontein. It was, however, repaired and returned to service. The Sigma no.801 was fairly reliable, being used for 138 days out of a possible 250 from August 1984 to July 1985 and its total was just under that for the Mercedes, at 39,271km. There were considerable problems with noise from the power drive to the auxiliary equipment and in service this vehicle ran with a distinctly loud whine, this drawing unfavourable comments from drivers and passengers. The Springfield/AEG no.804 broke down while in service on 26 October 1983 and had to be towed back to the depot. It managed to run on only 61 days in the period August 1984 to July 1985 and had a total of only 12,986km on its clock by the end of the project. Ansaldo no.802 notched up only 7,160km in all and, having been off the road for the second half of 1983, ran on only 27 days in 1984-5. The Toshiba-equipped no.803 ran a total of 11,627km, being laid up from February to July 1985. The single-deckers did not do any better, achieving only 10,735km (no.805) and 10,850km (no.804), and the former had problems with the chopper control equipment. Overall average availability was only 28%, while the old trolleybuses were still returning about 30,000km per year.

It had been intended to run two modern Mercedes 0305 double-deck motorbuses on the service alongside the trolleybuses, to gain comparative data on such matters as fuel consumption, maintenance costs, reliability, passenger and crew reaction and pollution. If this was indeed done, the results were not made public. They might have made interesting reading. Some of the experimental double-deckers did run on other routes from time to time, but always on "European" services.

Both public and operator became increasingly frustrated as the months went on and there was little sign of improvement. Matters had become so bad in the early months of 1983 that the project's steering committee gave the manufacturers until May of that year to bring the trolleybuses to a serviceable condition – or withdraw them. It was agreed that the experiment should run for three years from the starting date, after which either side could give the other three months' notice of its intention to withdraw. There was some improvement, but by mid-1984 operation had become spasmodic, and from April 1985 very few trolleybuses were to be seen on the demonstration route. At its meeting in October 1985, the City Council decided to terminate the project and gave the Department of Transport the requisite three months' notice. As no buyers could be found for the vehicles, no.800 was converted to a motorbus and the others were scrapped except for single-decker no.806, which was set aside for preservation in the James Hall Museum of Transport as the city's last new trolleybus. However, it is not there now and it is not certain if it still exists.

One of the main reasons for the problems was that the vehicles incorporated a great deal of new technology, but, with one exception, there were no local specialists who could deal with faults and experts, and, sometimes, replacement parts, had to be flown in from Europe when things went wrong. With the benefit of hindsight, it can be said that it would have been better, and cheaper, to have used one type of trolleybus only, instead of having seven vehicles, each totally different from the others. This diversity naturally increased the overall cost, but even so, it appeared that trolleybuses were simply too dear and that a 38-strong fleet, the minimum thought necessary to operate a service, would require a grant of R6.7 million from central government, and there was no likelihood that this would be forthcoming. The management of the JTD seemed to be lukewarm about the scheme and there were also political difficulties. The otherwise-admirable Progressive Party, which had a strong following in the northern part of the route in Berea, had in the past been anti-trolleybus, and, although one of its councillors was now chairman of the transport committee, the voters were perhaps not convinced by his assertion that "1973 (the oil crisis) had changed everything". Probably because of apartheid, the world's transport press took very little notice of the experiment and it has in consequence been difficult to piece the story together. Politics and finance seem to have had more to do with the failure of the project than the design of the vehicles themselves, though some of these were certainly disappointing. It is clear that the two which were relatively successful, nos.800 and 801, were those based on existing motorbus chassis, one of which had been giving excellent service in Johannesburg since 1977 and the other of which was proving itself in the strenuous conditions of operation in Hong Kong. The most constructive comment which could be made was that a great deal of useful technical information had been gained from the project.

It was all very disappointing for a project which had been begun with such high hopes. With a little more perseverance, the story of this and thus of other systems could well have been different.

Operation of trolleybuses on other services had finally ended on 8 June 1984. However, it was to be another two years before the final trolleybus ran in the streets of

Johannesburg. In 1986 the City Council decided to commemorate the golden jubilee of trolleybus operation and, as the overhead and power supply on the demonstration route were still functional, one of the 1958 BUTs, no.1649, was reactivated, given a special paint scheme and operated on the route from September to November of that year. It was then placed in the James Hall Museum for preservation, along with 1948 BUT no.600. Another BUT, no.589 was originally set aside for preservation in Britain, along with an AEC Regent V motorbus and one of the three-axle Guy Arab double-deck buses of 1958. Owing to problems of logistics and finance, this plan fell through and the vehicles were instead donated to the museum which had been established at Midmar Dam near Pietermaritzburg. This closed in 1989 and the vehicles have fortunately found a new home with the Durban Historical Transport Museum.

Apart from the vehicles used on the demonstration project, livery throughout the trolleybus era in Johannesburg was deep cherry red and cream with silver roof. Until the last few years, the vehicles were maintained in immaculate condition and, although advertisements were carried, these were always confined to a few parts of the bodies and the trolleybuses were not at any time allowed to become mobile hoardings.

Johannesburg was by far the largest operator of double-deckers outwith the British Isles. In all a total of 213 trolleybuses, all double-deckers, were owned, though not all, of course, at one time. To these should be added five double-deckers and two single-deckers from the demonstration project. It was the only system on which double-deckers catering for different races were operated along the same sets of overhead wires, a practice which gave rise to operating difficulties where loadings were of different densities. On the Dunkeld service, numbers of black passengers were considerably greater than those of "Europeans" and this caused

The trolleybuses were always immaculately turned out and here four cleaners are maintaining that tradition with no.17, still fairly new. (Les Pivnic collection)

delays to trolleybuses catering for the latter which caught up with and were then delayed by their opposite numbers. To attempt to cope with this problem, a siding was constructed

In the revised style of painting adopted in the 1960s, no.576 heads for the city centre in 1962, working on service 67 from Melville, and followed by BUT no.655 and another first series vehicle in the former livery. These are both working as service 98 from the Milner Park exhibition ground. (Pam Eaton)

An animated scene at Dunkeld terminus in 1962, as no.567 on "Non European" service prepares to negotiate the turning circle, one of the large trolleybuses makes for the city on the left and an AEC Regent V motorbus comes in on the right. The 2 was Johannesburg's most frequent "Non European" service. (Pam Eaton)

at Englewood Drive to allow southbound trolleybuses to overtake, but this did not really cure the problem, and in the end the only solution found was conversion of European working to motorbus operation, this occurring in June 1972. It was one of the longest-lived of such systems, its life of just over fifty years (albeit with intermittent running at the end)

No.707 waiting to leave the Frazer Street bus station for Parktown N. in August 1977. (Author)

being exceeded in Britain by only Bradford, Rotherham and the Tees-side Board. Finally, Johannesburg was the only British-type system in Africa to expand considerably in the 1950s and to experiment with a new generation of trolleybuses in the 1980s.

> **Total number of double-deck trolleybuses operated: 213 + 5 on demonstration project: 218**

PRETORIA

The last South African city to adopt the trolleybus was Pretoria. In transport matters this rather quiet city had always lagged behind the others; horse trams were operated from 1897 and municipal electric trams began service only in 1910. The vehicles used were all single-deckers.

In 1937 the City Council decided to replace the trams by trolleybuses and on 15 September 1938 an order was placed for 34 Leyland TB7 trolleybuses, ten of those to be double-deckers. Based on experience of the trams, it was assumed that single-deckers would be able to cope with most of the services, the double-deckers helping out at times of higher demand.

All the vehicles had Metro-Cammell bodies, built in that firm's Birmingham factory, those on the double-deckers being very similar to those recently supplied by that firm to Johannesburg, apart from the lack of the front exit fitted to those. The tender documents had specified that they would have to be able to cope with Pretoria's high summer humidity and the possibility of flash floods after heavy thunderstorms. Internally they were finished to a high standard and had curtains which could be drawn across the saloon windows to shield passengers from the summer sun. The double-deckers were numbered 150-159 and seated 56 passengers, (30/26). They had GEC equipment and GEC motors with regenerative

braking, as in Johannesburg, but it was found that this feature was not of any great benefit and it was not repeated on later orders. The single-deckers, which had the same equipment, seated 38 passengers in bodies of rather boxy and old-fashioned appearance.

The last trams in normal service ran, without ceremony, on 31 July 1939. However, the collapse of a bridge as a result of a sudden and very violent storm delayed the opening of the trolleybus service and also allowed the operation of an official "last tram". The Corporation had hoped that the occasion would pass unnoticed but the citizens seem to have had some affection for their trams and public opinion forced the authorities to provide a ceremonial last run to Pretoria West on Saturday 19 August. Trolleybus overhead had already been mounted above the tram wires and it was then a simple matter to cut these down and allow the trolleybuses to enter service. In fact the conversion went ahead so well that the first trolleybus ran on the Sunday afternoon, being "piloted" by Councillor F. Hopf, chairman of the Trading Committee and a long-time advocate of trolleybuses. The sections converted to trolleybus operation, 15 route miles in total, were the east-west main line which ran in a straight line along Church Street for six miles, with its branch through Sunnyside to Jorissen Street, and short half-mile links south to the station and north to the Zoo. An extension beyond the tram terminus in the east took the trolleybuses to Brooklyn. The attractive branch to the Union Buildings, which ran on reserved track, was not converted to trolleybus operation, perhaps because it was feared that trolleybus overhead would spoil the view of this dignified structure. A new depot was built in Boom Street to house the trolleybuses and the municipality's motorbus fleet of 24 petrol- and 31 diesel-engined motorbuses, but this had not been completed when the trolleybuses arrived, and the new vehicles had to be stored outside the tram depot in van der Walt Street. Just three weeks later South Africa entered the second world war and immediately demand for transport in Pretoria rose to

No.151 in Church Square, in original livery. (B.T. Cooke, courtesy Alan Murray)

Post-war BUT double-decker no.193 at Colbyn terminus about 1960. (John Grant-Silver)

Sunbeam no.167 at Brooklyn terminus. (John Grant-Silver)

Daimler no.178 awaiting departure from the central terminus of Church Square for Hatfield on service 1. (John Grant-Silver)

unprecedented levels, with increased numbers of civil servants and defence personnel being based in the city. The City Council was soon to regret that it had not bought more double-deckers and all post-war deliveries were for this type of trolleybus.

Passengers took to the new service enthusiastically and an increase of 20% in the number of passengers carried on routes concerned, by comparison with tramway days. In its first year of operation, there was a profit of £4,810. It was decided to extend the system to Capital Park and Riviera and to link the Sunnyside and Brooklyn termini. Ten further Leyland double-deckers were ordered. Owing to war-time conditions, these were not built and the extensions had to be postponed.

The system expanded considerably in the immediate post-war years, with four new routes and several extensions of existing lines. The West End terminus sprouted no fewer than four branches, while in the east the main line was extended to Colbyn. There was also a new line from a point on the Sunnyside route through Loftus Versveld to Hatfield on the line to Brooklyn. In the north, new routes brought the overhead wires to Rietfontein and Wonderboom South via Riviera and to Parktown via Capital Park. These extensions brought the network to its maximum extent of 28 miles, worked as nine services, all of which terminated in Church Square. To work these and replace some of the single-deckers, orders were placed for 30 additional double-deckers, plus those ten ordered in 1940 but not constructed. These last materialised in 1950 as BUT 9611T vehicles, nos.190-199. There were also twelve Sunbeam F4s, nos.160-171 and 18 Daimler CTM4s, nos.172-189, these last being the only

Daimler No.187 outbound for Brooklyn has just turned into Duncan Street from Lynwood Road, in January 1970. (Roger M. Perry)

Daimler trolleybuses to run in South Africa and indeed the only Daimlers to be exported. The BUTs had 56-seat Metro-Cammell bodies, of pre-war design, one being completed in Britain and the others by Bus Bodies in Port Elizabeth. The others had bodies by BMS, similar to those being supplied to Johannesburg and Durban, but one bay shorter. Seating capacity was 32/28. The Daimlers had control equipment and motors by Metropolitan-Vickers. All were two-axle vehicles,

A rear view of no.187, which has just left Brooklyn and is inbound on Duncan Street, January 1970. (Roger M. Perry)

fitted with trolley retrievers, Pretoria being the only city in South Africa to make use of these. After the single-deckers had been withdrawn, these new vehicles also replaced the original double-deckers, the last of which ran in 1960.

The final batch of ten trolleybuses to be acquired by Pretoria had several "lasts" to their credit, although this would not have been realised when they entered service in 1960. They were the last double-deckers to be built by Sunbeam, the last three axle trolleybuses to be built in Britain and the last trolleybuses to be acquired by any South African system. They were impressive Sunbeam S7As and had bodies by J. Brockhouse (formerly BMS) and were numbered 140-149. They had a single forward door and 3+2 seating on the upper deck allowed the high seating capacity of 82 (49/33). To allow possible use in one-person operation, the driver's cab was not partitioned off from the passengers. Unfortunately they had a relatively short life, as the run-down of the system began in 1963, after which trolleybuses operated only on weekdays and Saturday mornings. The Parktown service was withdrawn in 1968 owing to highway construction and complete closure came on 21 February 1972. Attempts to interest Johannesburg in the Sunbeams failed and they were all prematurely broken up. Daimler 177 has been preserved in the James Hall museum and it was hoped to bring back sister vehicle 187 to Britain for preservation, but due to problems in transporting the bus to a port, the scheme fell through.

The livery first used in Pretoria was a dignified one of blue-grey, with dark blue window surrounds and black lining. The post-war vehicles were painted grey with red dashes and red front and rear roof domes, but they were liberally adorned with advertisements which spoiled the general effect and some were turned out in overall advertising livery. One, advertising the services of a building society, masqueraded as a house, complete with neatly pointed brickwork. The 1960 Sunbeams had an orange-red livery with cream window surrounds and a cream streamline V below the windscreen. Although they did carry

No.140 on service 3 at Sunnyside. (John Grant-Silver)

advertisements, these were applied in a more restrained manner. Pretoria was the only trolleybus system to carry the undertaking's title in full, in English and Afrikaans on the sides of the vehicles. The former was always applied on the nearside the latter on the offside.

This system always operated on strictly segregated lines and the trolleybuses were used by "white" passengers only.

Total number of double-deckers operated: 60

PORT ELIZABETH

As transport in this city was run by a company which was part of the Cape Tramways group, it is not surprising that plans were made to convert its trams to trolleybuses. Agreement was reached with the municipality about this in 1940 and this was ratified by Private Ordinance no.11 in 1941. The war, of course, had by now made any implementation of these plans impossible, but the company invited Weymann to prepare a design for a three-axle central-entrance double-deck trolleybus, with three separate saloons, which would have fitted in with the city's policy of segregating passengers on the same vehicle. Owing to the rise in costs in the post-war period, the plans were abandoned and the last trams were replaced by motorbuses on 3 December 1948.

LOURENÇO MARQUES

A double-deck Karrier (which would have been a Karrier-Clough) is reported to have run in this city on demonstration in 1930. Nothing further is known of this trolleybus and it is not mentioned in the history of the tramway system. In 1932 a delegation from Lourenço Marques visited Bloemfontein to study the operation of trolleybuses and they would no doubt have seen no.5. It may be that the double-decker just bought by Bloemfontein was shipped via Lourenço Marques (see above) and it could conceivably have made a short demonstration run using tramway track and overhead. In any event, the trial, if it did take place, was without result and, when the city's trams were withdrawn in 1936, they were replaced by single-deck motorbuses.

There have also been reports that Doncaster Corporation no.22 was shipped to Johannesburg in 1930 for demonstration purposes, later returning to its native city. This is not confirmed by any local source. Once again there may be confusion with Bloemfontein no.5. Neither report can now be confirmed.

BOKSBURG & GERMISTON

For the sake of completeness, brief mention may be made here of these two systems, although neither operated double-deckers. Boksburg is about 16 miles east of Johannesburg and on 25 March 1914 it opened South Africa's first trolleybus operation. It consisted of about four miles of route, with a main line from the town centre to Vogelfontein and two short branches. This was installed by the Railless Electric Traction Company Ltd, who also built the six front-entrance single-deckers to work it. These were 28-seaters and were tested in Leeds prior to shipment. The system was hopelessly unprofitable and closed at some time in 1918. Most of the overhead equipment was bought by Johannesburg and used on tramway extensions.

Germiston followed in August of the same year with a Cedes-Stoll installation, running from the Malvern terminus of the Johannesburg trams for 4.86 miles to Victoria Lake. Ten rear-entrance single-deckers were employed, along with one trailer and there was also a tower wagon. Working expenses exceeded receipts by a considerable margin and the war made it difficult to obtain spare parts. This system also closed in 1918.

It should be noted that South African English often referred to the vehicle as a "Trollybus". In Afrikaans it was a "Trembus" (Trambus). Bloemfontein, Boksburg and Cape Town generally used the term "Trackless Tram".

Bibliography

The British Trolleybus. G. Lumb. Ian Allan Ltd., Surrey, 1995

Track and Trackless. P.R. Coates. C. Struik, Cape Town, 1976

Tram and Trolley in Africa. M. Pabst. Röhr Verlag, Krefeld, 1989

Johannesburg Tramways. T. Spit, revised and enlarged by B. Patton. Light Railway Transport League, London, 1976.

Cape Trams from Horse to Diesel. Fraser Gill and Associates, Cape Town, 1961

Omnibus Magazine no.93, June 1955 (Durban)

Trolleybus Magazine no.61, November 1971 (Durban)

Classic Bus nos.25 (Cape Town), 31 (Durban), 42 (Johannesburg)

Trolleybus – Journal of British Trolleybus Society no.32, August 1988 (Johannesburg experiment)

Unpublished material by J. Grant-Silver on Pretoria

Material supplied to the author by Johannesburg Municipal Transport.

Johannesburg Trolleybus Reports. Unpublished papers by M.I. Baxter, November 1981, June and August 1982 and 1985

Johannesburg Trolleybus Demonstration Project – Operation of Prototype Trolleybuses, 1983/4. unpublished reports by Roger M. Perry

Newspaper articles on trolleybus demonstration project, 1980 onwards.

Hong Kong Buses, volume one. M.J. Davis. DTS Publishing, Croydon, 1994

Buses Illustrated, no.53, July 1959 (Cape Town), no.64, July 1960 (London's SA classes)

Buses, no.491, February 1996 (Johannesburg no.801)

Newsletters of the National Trolleybus Association (Johannesburg news)

G.E.C. Journal, August 1942. (Pretoria)

South African Transport, September 1975, May and December 1976. G. Shields. South Africa's Trolleybuses.

Port Elizabeth Tramways. Graham Shields. Port Elizabeth Tramways, Port Elizabeth, 1979

South Africa. PMP Video, 2001. (Films of trolleybuses in Durban, Johannesburg and Pretoria)

The Weymann Story, Part One, 1923-1945. J.A. Senior, A. Townsin and J. Banks. Venture Publications, Glossop, 2002.

Addresses of museums

The James Hall Transport Museum is located in Pioneer Park, Turffontein, in the southern suburbs of Johannesburg

The Durban Historical Transport Museum is in Argyle Road in the city. Telephone 083 289 0509. Postal address PO Box 11715, Marine Parade, Durban 4056

The "Green Goddess" as preserved at the St. Kilda museum. (Author)

AUSTRALIA

ADELAIDE

In the capital of South Australia, the transport system was in the 1930s operated by the Municipal Tramways Trust (MTT). Under the leadership of W.G. Gooodman, Chief Engineer from 1907 and General Manager from the following year, it became one of Australia's most progressive undertakings. The possibility of running trolleybuses was first discussed as far back as January 1912, but nothing came of this idea. The MTT began motorbus operation in 1914 and acquired its first double-deck motorbuses on 4 November 1927, when it bought a fleet of 28 Garford CB open-top vehicles from South Australian Railways. These normal control buses had been imported form the USA in 1926 and given bodies, seating 33/23 passengers, in SAR's Islington workshops. In the MTT fleet they were numbered 201-228 and proved to be successful in service, lasting until March 1950. From 1935 onwards, a fleet of eleven enclosed double-deckers was built up.

The first trolleybus to run in the city was in fact a conversion from one of the Garfords. In 1932 no.216 was converted into a trolleybus and used on an experimental service along the single track and very lightly-trafficked tram line, 2.73 miles in length, from Payneham to Paradise, in the north east suburbs, in off-peak hours, when only one vehicle was required to maintain the service. The upper deck seats, stairs and rear platform were removed and a front entrance was fitted. A small tower to support the trolley booms was placed on the floor of the former upper deck and an English Electric DK 130 80hp motor was installed. As a trolleybus, there was seating for 22 passengers. The cost of conversion was stated to be £1,200, excluding the book value of the "old bus". Trials began in March 1932 and the first passengers were carried, on an experimental basis, on 18 April. Regular passenger service began on 2 May. The trolleybus overhead was placed alongside that for the trams and turning was effected by a loop at Paradise and a reversing Y at Payneham. Between Payneham and Hackney depot only the positive pole was used on tramway overhead, with a skate trailing in the tram track providing for the negative return, except for a short section of normal trolleybus overhead to negotiate the corner of Hackney

road and North Terrace, about a ¼-mile from the depot. No.216 carried a novel livery of green and cream and was known as the "Green Goddess". The service was judged a success, although a full tram service was restored to Paradise on 12 August 1934, trolleybus service having finished on the previous day. No.216 was placed in store.

In 1933 Sir William Goodman, as he had become in 1932, visited Europe. He attended conferences in Oslo, Copenhagen and Stockholm and visited England, where he inspected the latest in motorbus, tramway and trolleybus technology. He returned to Adelaide on 4 November.

On 5 September 1937 a permanent trolleybus installation was begun, with a route replacing the bus service from Light Square/Morphett Street in the city to the south-eastern suburb of Tusmore. On 3 April of the following year, after trials which had begun on 19 January, the line was extended to Port Adelaide, where it bifurcated to serve Semaphore and Largs. This was again a replacement for motorbus operation which had replaced the former local tram network, which had had no connexion with the main city system. From the MTT's advertising material for the opening of this extension, it is clear that only Largs trolleybuses ran through to Tusmore, those from Semaphore turning back at the eastern end of the city centre, at Dequetteville Terrace. The conversion was evidently a success, to the point where, according to *The Advertiser* newspaper, the trolleybuses had to be supplemented by diesel buses. On 18 January 1952 the official opening of an extension of the Tusmore service to Beaumont was held and regular service began on 20 January. On 12 October of the same year the trams to Linden Park were replaced by trolleybuses, this being the first such conversion in Adelaide. There was an extension of about half a mile beyond the former tram terminus. On 17 May 1953 two new lines were opened in the eastern suburbs to Burnside and

No.411 in Rundle Street in the city centre in 1939. (MTT, courtesy Dr J. Radcliffe)

No.408 in the red and silver livery in Rundle Street in the city centre in 1957. (Dr J. Radcliffe collection)

Erindale, to replace buses which had themselves replaced trams on 25 May 1952. All these termini are in the south-east of the city and the extensions were essentially branches off the main line. This brought the total route mileage to 22.55. Regular trolleybus service ceased on Friday 12 July 1963, single-deck three-door motorbuses taking over on the following day.

Depots were located at Hackney and Port Adelaide. The former was shared with trams and, latterly, motorbuses, and was reconstructed in 1954/5. The latter had been a tram depot and was rebuilt for the introduction of trolleybus services to Port Adelaide in 1938. Its layout was somewhat awkward and at night some vehicles had to be parked on the exit ramp, their wheels chocked to prevent a runaway. A prefabricated annexe was opened in June 1944 to cope with the growth in the fleet and the whole complex was rebuilt in 1955/6.

When the war had finished, planning was begun on the conversion of the motorbus routes to Cheltenham and Largs North. By the end of 1946 all the poles and span wires had been erected on the former and many poles were in place on the latter. It had been hoped to begin trolleybus service in October 1946 but shortages of materials led to postponements and in the end work ceased. In 1951 it was then decided not to proceed with this and the poles and wires which had been erected were taken down.

For the opening of the Tusmore service, twenty trolleybuses were ordered early in 1936, nos.401-420. These were built by AEC (661T) and had bodies by the local firm of J.A. Lawton and Sons of North Terrace, Adelaide. They seated 33/26, with 25 standees allowed. The cost of these trolleybuses was £3,517 each. They had 90hp Metropolitan-Vickers motors, manufactured in Australia by Australian General Electric and English Electric control equipment. A front exit, with an air-operated folding door, was fitted. An MTT equipment summary gives the length over bumpers as 29ft 10¾in and width as 8ft 3¼in. Unladen weight was 8¾ tons. It would appear that both here and in Sydney, trolleybus bodies which were 8ft wide were used on chassis designed for vehicles 7ft 6in wide. The first was delivered to Hackney depot on 3 July 1937 and the first trial runs between that point and Tusmore, using no.409, took place exactly one week later. The new service was treated as a prestige operation, and a standard piece of equipment on each trolleybus was a dust pan and brush, which conductors were expected to use to good effect at termini. City stores also featured the splendid new service in their advertisements prior to the opening of the line.

As mentioned above, it was found that twenty vehicles were insufficient to run the full service and ten further trolleybuses, nos.421-430, were delivered in the autumn of 1938.

No.428 at Hackney depot about 1956. (Noel Reed, courtesy Dr J. Radcliffe)

No.431 in Hackney Road when fairly new. (MTT, courtesy Dr J. Radcliffe)

They were almost identical to those of the first batch but were slightly more expensive at £3,661 each. They could, however, be distinguished by the fixed windows at the front of the upper deck, nos.401-420 having half-drop opening windows there. Not long after these vehicles entered service, the bodies on both batches began to show signs of structural weakness, and it was necessary to strengthen them with trusses and diagonal bracing in the front and rear lower saloon windows. By 30 June 1957 nos. 403/5/6/9/11 and 416 had already been withdrawn. The remainder were then placed in storage and nos.401/2 were sold off by 30 June 1958. The remaining 22 vehicles were briefly returned to traffic on 20 July 1958, to cover a motorbus shortage following a tram-bus conversion, but they were finally withdrawn in September of the same year. There is a possibility that this class may have been nicknamed "Arizona" by MTT staff but this cannot be confirmed; if correct, it would be interesting to know the source of the name, as no trolley-buses operated in that US state!

When the Tusmore service began, no.216 was taken out of store and reconstructed to grease the overhead wires. It thus managed to last into the era of preservation.

A further five trolleybus chassis were bought in 1938. These were three-axle Leylands (TTB4), which may have been imported by the Leyland agent in New South Wales, who was confident that a further order for such trolleybuses would soon be placed for Sydney. However, it is not clear from whom these buses were actually purchased by the MTT. The purchase was detailed in the report of the MTT to the Commissioner of Public Works (the responsible minister in the State government) of January 1939. Bodies, motors and control systems would be fitted when required. The report also stated that these

chassis had been bought "at a specially low price", but as the final cost was £4,597 per vehicle, they would seem not to have been much of a bargain! However, it may be that the war-time shortage of skilled craftsmen led to much overtime working to complete these vehicles. They were also mentioned by the Chief Engineer and General Manager in an article in January 1939, with the comment that they would not be needed for at least two years. They had bodywork by the MTT, using components obtained from Lawton, seating 37/29, and entered service in March 1942, numbered 431-435. A standing load of 27 was allowed in the lower saloon. Again an M-V 90hp motor was fitted. Dimensions are given in an MTT data sheet as length 31ft 0.5in and width 8ft 4in. Weight was 9.13 tons. On these vehicles, the front door was manually operated. These buses were not totally successful and were often out of traffic, although they seem to have

No.434 at Hackney Depot about 1956, with one of the Daimler double-deck motorbuses on the left. (Noel Reed, courtesy Dr J. Radcliffe)

No 435 at Kent Town in 1952. (MTT, courtesy Dr J. Radcliffe)

accumulated high mileages. It appears that they suffered from some chronic defect in the rear bogie, which the MTT was not willing to remedy. They were also unpopular with crews, possibly because of difficulties with the tight turning circles at Semaphore, Largs and Beaumont, and also because of their lack of power, which was especially marked on the climb from Tusmore to Beaumont. Nos.433 and 435 were withdrawn about June 1957 and the remainder were then placed in store, until withdrawn in 1958.

Later deliveries were all single-deckers. First came 26 Leyland two-axle TB5, nos.471-496, which were part of an order for Canton. These were diverted to Australia when war time conditions made it impossible for them to go there, and received bodies built by the MTT, nos.471-496. They entered service between 1942 and 1945. In Adelaide they were known as "wombats", their low-slung construction recalling that Australian mammal. In 1945 25 Sunbeam MF2B trolley-buses were ordered, followed by a further five in 1947. Post-war shortages meant that the chassis were not delivered until 1949/50. They were given bodies by J.A. Lawton and Sons, now of Kilkenny, and took the numbers 497-526, nos.497-500 later being renumbered 527-530. No.497 was the first to enter passenger service on 8 January 1952 and others followed at intervals until May 1953. No.526 operated a final tour, organised by the Australian Railway Historical Society, on 13 July 1963, with back-up from nos.515, 519 and 530. No.526 has since been preserved, along with Leyland no.488.

Initially all trolleybuses were painted in the tram livery of maroon (Tuscan red) with cream bands, these being separated from the red areas by thin black lines, and a silver roof, which in service seems to have dulled down to a light grey. During the war, no.404 was repainted white, to allow it to carry all-over advertising exhorting the citizens to subscribe firstly to war, then victory, loans. The front panel, however, advertised a local beer. Many of the AECs and all the "wombats" were later repainted silver with carnation red bands, the first double-decker to be so treated being

No.420 and Sunbeam 523 at the junction of Rundle Road, Hackney Road and Dequettville Terrace, Kent Town. The circle in the overhead, which allowed vehicles from either direction to proceed to Hackney depot, can be clearly seen. (Noel Reed, courtesy Dr J. Radcliffe)

no.426. None of the Leyland double-deckers received this paint scheme, which the Sunbeam single-deckers carried from new. Much of the paint scheme was by then obscured by advertising.

No route numbers were used, but there was a colour light code, for which four lights were provided, two on either side of the destination box. Unlike practice in other cities which have used such a code, only red and green lights – the green being a much lighter shade on the second batch of AECs – were used and the system became somewhat complicated after the post-war extensions. It was abandoned when the double-deckers were withdrawn. Additionally, on the double-deckers and Leyland single-deckers, a list of places served was carried on the waistband below the lower saloon windows. This practice was discontinued on vehicles which were repainted silver. An unusual feature of the trolleybus destination blinds was that the city centre was denoted as "Adelaide" whereas trams and motorbus blinds referred to this as "City". The trolleybus services were quite well integrated with local motorbus services and trolleybus destination blinds showed also the destination of the feeder buses with which there would be a connexion. Adelaide's trolley buses carried registration plates.

No.417 of the first batch to enter service has been preserved at the local tramway museum at St. Kilda, SA, its survival being due to its use as a mobile canteen when withdrawn. Renumbered S106, it was fitted with tables in the lower saloon and a hot water supply was installed on the upper deck. Each day it was driven from Hackney depot to its location at Kent Town, where a power box on an adjacent traction pole provided current for hot water. It last operated under its own power on 25 July 1963, after the trolleybus system had closed, and from then until it was withdrawn in 1967 it was towed around by a tractor unit. It is theoretically in running order but has not yet been restored to original condition. No.216, as used on the experimental line, is also at St. Kilda.

Leyland no.433 was initially preserved by an enthusiast in Adelaide and in 1991 was obtained by the Historic and Commercial Vehicle Association in Sydney. In a tow lasting three days, it was taken to the bus museum at Tempe garage in Sydney.

Total number of double-deckers operated: 35

SYDNEY

The transport system in the capital of New South Wales was in the 1930s operated as the Department of Road Transport and Tramways. This was a Crown Corporation, set up by the Transport (Division of Functions) Act of 1932. At that time the city had the second-largest tram systems in the then British empire. By 1934 it had also begun to build up a small fleet of double-deck motorbuses, which was later to expand to be one of the largest of such fleets outwith the British Isles.

On 22 January 1934 an experimental trolleybus service was inaugurated between Museum Station in the city, at the junction of Elizabeth and Liverpool Streets, and Potts Point via Kings Cross, in the inner eastern suburbs, using two single-deckers, nos.1 and 2. These were AEC 663T three-axle vehicles. The bodywork on no.1 was by Park Royal Vehicles, the bus being imported complete into Australia, while no.2 was bodied locally by H. McKenzie.

On 30 September of the same year the line was extended

Only just off the ship which had brought it from Britain, the trolleybus which would become no.3 is seen on the Sydney dockside. (V. Solomons collection)

Now painted into DRTT livery, no.3 is on an inbound working to Wylde Street in 1934, sharing the road with some very vintage motor cars. (V. Solomons collection)

buses placed in service by Bradford and Southend Corporations. The importation of a vehicle of such an experimental nature was certainly a bold venture by the DRTT, but it should be remembered that at this time, Sydney saw itself, at least in transport terms, as basically a British city and would have wanted to follow current British practice. Initially the DRTT referred to the vehicles as "trackless trolley buses" but the adjective was soon dropped. It appears that two other chassis were imported at the same time as no.3, but these were placed in store. In 1936 the second chassis was given a body identical to that of no.3, by Syd. Wood of Bankstown, a local firm which built some double-deck bodies for the city's motorbuses. It entered service as no.4 on 8 April and was used to improve the frequency of the service. The third chassis was bodied later in 1936, also by Wood, with the same design of bodywork. It had been intended that, as no.5, this vehicle would be used, in conjunction with the existing steam trams, on the new line in the suburbs, at Kogarah. In the event, it joined its counterparts on the Potts Point service on 24 June 1937. The bodybuilder was obviously quite proud of these vehicles and featured no.4 in advertising. An unusual feature of these

inwards to Town Hall station, via Park, George and Bathurst Streets, as part of a further extension to Central Railway, which in the event did not materialise. This line was complementary to, not a replacement of, existing tram services. When the extension opened, the first double-decker was placed in service, as no.3. This was an AEC Q-type (761T) trolleybus, which was imported complete to Australia. It had a Park Royal body of composite construction, seating 33/30 and was in all respects identical to the double-deck Q trolley-

In this busy scene at King's Cross about 1937, no. 4 jostles for road space with some streamlined cars from the US and two R1 class trams on the Watson's Bay service. (V. Solomons collection)

No. 4, inbound to the city, negotiates the intersection of William, College and Park Streets on 28 February 1948. This crossing was notorious for dewirements of outbound trolleybuses, as these had first to cross under the inbound wires then under four successive insulators, first under the Park Street tramway overhead, then under that for College Street. Bitter experience, especially with the single-deckers, made sure that drivers took this crossing at very low speed. (Noel Reed)

trolleybuses was the placing of the fleet number in the box above the destination box, originally intended for the service number. Like the city's trams, the trolleybuses did not use service numbers.

Length of the Q class vehicles was 26ft 0in and width 7ft 7in. No.3 weighed 6.65 tons, but the Syd. Wood bodied vehicles were slightly heavier, at 7.24 tons. All three had English Electric control equipment and an EE 87hp self-ventilated motor of type 405-7C, this being mounted on the offside of the frame, in the middle of the chassis. The contactors were also mounted under the floor, in water- and splash-proof cases. To accommodate the numerous crossings with tramway overhead and allow use of this on depot journeys, these vehicles were fitted with trolley wheels, rather than the more usual shoes. No.3 initially had a tramway type lifeguard, activated by a stainless steel trigger bar and there was provision for a similar fitment on no.4, but in the event this was not used. Emergency doors were provided at the rear of both the lower and upper saloons. Nos.3-5 cost £3,375, £2,833 and £2,759 respectively.

Another unusual feature of this line was that arrangement of the overhead was non-standard, in that the positive wire was closest to the kerb. As detailed in DRTT Circular no.1 of 1934, this arrangement allowed trolley-buses, on depot journeys along Bayswater Road, between Kings Cross and Rushcutter's Bay depot, to use the tramway positive overhead with a single negative wire for current return strung between the two tramway wires. Within the depot, a turntable was

provided in the area which had housed the power station for the cable tramway which had been used between 1894 and 1905. Manoeuvring the trolleybuses on and off the turntable required the use of jumper cables.

In March 1948 no.3 collided with the wall outside the Australian Museum in College Street and was so badly damaged that it was written off. On 12 April of the same year the trolleybuses were replaced by motorbuses, on what was initially described as a temporary basis. However, in 1949 the conversion was made permanent. In August of that year the two remaining double-deckers followed the two single-deckers to Kogarah, the trolley wheels being replaced by sliding shoe collectors on all vehicles. They proved to be unpopular with passengers and crews on that system and saw only limited use. The greatest problem with nos. 4 and 5 was caused by the regenerative braking, as there were not always

No.5, as rebuilt, alongside a contemporary AEC Regent motorbus. (Noel Reed)

No.20, in original condition, outside the depot on 2 August 1952. (Noel Reed)

operators (including Auckland!) having failed, they were sold in March and April 1957, after all electrical equipment had been removed at Randwick workshops. No.4 became a feature in a children's playground and no.5 a beach hut. Both have since been scrapped. It was a great pity that it was not possible to preserve one of these unique vehicles. Only two other examples of the type were operated in Britain – one each in Bradford and Southend – and the DRTT deserved much credit for their willingness to experiment with it. There were also three double-deck motor-buses of the same type, the first of which arrived just after no.3.

The second Sydney trolleybus line was a completely different operation. In 1887 a steam tram line was constructed between Kogarah railway station, Sandringham and Sans Souci. On 1 March 1926 the Illawarra railway line was electrified to Oatley and on 20 December was linked to the new City Railway with a new station named Central, adjacent to the main line station. This led to a great increase in traffic and the steam trams, the last to be operated by the DRTT, were hard pressed to act as feeders to the new trains. Local councils began to agitate for better facilities, that in Kogarah requesting electrification of the tram line, while that of Rockdale suggested replacing it with trolley-buses. A newspaper report in the *Sydney Morning Herald* on 23 July 1935 said that motor buses would replace the trams,

sufficient other trolleybuses on the road to absorb the current thus generated. As a result, they could be used only at peak hours, and then one only. No.4 was not used after 1953 but despite the problems, no.5 was rebuilt in 1953 and was then given sliding windows to the upper deck, diagonal bracing to the lower saloon windows and a new livery. It was still not considered to be a success in its new home and no work was done on no.4, which saw scarcely any further service. The narrow bodies restricted the width of the gangway, to the annoyance of conductors, and the single doorway became a bottleneck at Kogarah station, when passengers wanted to alight as quickly as possible to catch their train. Both vehicles were withdrawn in 1956 and, attempts to sell them to other

The Hotel Rockdale and the three-axle trolleybus were both products of the 1930s. A passenger appears to be boarding by the front exit! (Robert Clarke collection, courtesy Noel Reed)

but on 14 March 1936 the same newspaper reported that trolleybuses would be used. Tenders for the supply of chassis had actually been issued on 21 July 1935. Orders were subsequently placed for eleven Leyland TTB4 chassis (nos. 6-16) and ten AEC 664T chassis (nos.17-26). Metropolitan-Vickers 201-DT 90hp motors were fitted and control equipment was by English Electric.

The Commissioner for Road Transport and Tramways, S.A. Maddocks, had visited Britain in 1935 and had attended the opening of trolleybus routes 657 and 667 in London on 27 October 1935, the first tram to trolleybus conversion under the auspices of London Transport. He had mentioned the possibility of trolleybuses operating in New South Wales and said that he foresaw a great future for this form of transport, adding, rather cautiously, that he was unsure how far this would extend. Probably as a result of contact made during this visit, trolleybus specifications were obtained from London Transport. Subsequently on 20 May 1936 tenders were issued for the supply of one two-axle trolleybus body (no.5) and 21 bodies for three-axle chassis.

For the bodywork it was decided to take as a model the vehicles then being placed in service in Newcastle-upon-Tyne. The order for the metal-framed bodies for the three-axle vehicles went to a Sydney firm, Ritchie Brothers, and deliveries began on 19 April 1937. Length was 30ft 6in, width 8ft 0in and unladen weight 8.7 tons. Seating capacity was 33/27 and an unlimited number of standees was permitted on the lower deck. On the upper deck, there was a seat for three at the front, ahead of the forward stair, and three single seats beside it on the nearside. Apart from another seat for three behind the rear stair, all other seats were for two persons. In the lower deck, there were eight forward-facing double seats, one longitudinal seat for five on the offside and a similar seat for six on the nearside. The trolleybuses were

handsome and spacious vehicles, with dual doors and dual stairs. The folding door at the front was manually operated and was often left in the open position when the vehicle was in service. Normally the forward stairs and doors were used as exits, but at Kogarah station passengers were allowed to alight front and rear. Since the open rear platform would still be accessible even if the trolleybus fell over on the nearside, an emergency exit was provided only at the rear of the upper deck. As on vehicles running in Britain, a full width cab was provided for the driver and a contemporary advertisement by Australian GEC mentioned that, while this seemed to be a waste of space, the extra room would be an advantage in driver training – it was suggested that there would be a need for many additional drivers "as this type of transport will become prominent in Sydney". The internal finish was to a slightly higher standard than that of contemporary DRTT motorbuses. Half-drop windows were fitted on both decks, whereas motorbuses had horizontally-sliding windows. Interior lighting was excellent. Interior panelling was covered in dark green rexine and seats were covered in leather of the same colour. Mouldings were of polished timber. Obviously proud of its new vehicles, the DRTT issued an instruction to traffic staff that baskets of fish and prawns were not to be carried on board trolleybuses! In the early days at least, a broom, dust pan and duster were part of every Kogarah trolleybus's equipment and conductors were expected to use these to keep the interior clean. Until 1939 smoking was allowed in both saloons, thereafter on the upper deck only. Sliding shoe collectors were fitted to these buses. However, no.24 was briefly fitted with trolley wheels to allow it to pose for an official photograph on the Potts Point line at College Street, in company with R1 class tram no.1984 and motorbus MO'572, to show all that was modern in Sydney's transport. The Leyland chassis are reported to

There could scarcely have been a greater contrast than that between steam tram motor no.84A and the new trolleybus and it was not surprising that Kogarah was en fête for the opening of the service on 4 July 1937. (V. Solomons collection)

No.19 at Kogarah station in 1959. (V. Solomons)

have cost £2,107 each and those of the AECs £2,070 each. The bodies cost £1,043. However, the DRTT Accountant's ledger gives the total cost as £3,236 per vehicle. Ritchie Bros. erected a new large shed to handle this order. There was also a suggestion that they would assemble a further 60-passenger body for special purposes, but nothing further is known of this.

The line basically replaced the steam tram line, with some variations to allow more flexible working, but was extended inwards to Rockdale from Kogarah station. It was operated under regulations issued by the Governor-in-Council, under the Transport Act of 1930, on 25 June

A rear view of the same vehicle at the same location. (V. Solomons)

1937. Throughout this document it was referred to as a "trackless trolley" line. Initially a maximum speed of 25mph was allowed for these buses on the Kogarah system, but this was soon limited to 20mph by a departmental circular of 4 July 1937, thus bringing them into line with those at Potts Point.

The official opening of the service by the State Premier, Bertram Stevens, took place on 3 July 1937, using nos.7,17 and 23 in that order, the first of these being decorated with bunting and the Australian and British flags. After Mr. Stevens had cut ribbons at both Kogarah and Rockdale, invited guests toured the system and later took tea at Sans Souci. The steam trams continued to run throughout the day and the last left Kogarah, packed to beyond capacity, at 01.00 on 4 July. Public operation began on that day. This was certainly the only occasion on which British-style trolley-buses replaced a steam tram line and it is doubtful if this

occurred to any extent elsewhere.

The service was subject to very heavy peak hour loadings, with two or three trolleybuses meeting each train from the city in the evening peak. By contrast, only three trolleybuses were required to maintain the service in off-peak hours, when the frequency came down to 15 minutes. Normally, 16 vehicles were sufficient to maintain all schedules, but the General Manager stated that 21 had been provided to cope with holiday traffic to Sans Souci and Lady Robinson's beach. However, an article in the June 1937 issue of the magazine *Transportation* suggested that the six additional vehicles (obviously assuming that no, 5 would also be at Kogarah) would be retained for future services. The depot, which was built new for the trolleybuses, was in Ritchie Street, Ramsgate, although it was often referred to as "Kogarah".

Unfortunately the Commissioner concerned was jailed for

Two trolleybuses, with no.8 on the right, inbound in Rocky Point Road, Ramsgate. In the distance a third vehicle emerges from the Campbell Street loop and is having its booms placed on the outbound wires to allow it to proceed to the depot or Sans Souci. (L. Manny, V. Solomons collection)

18 months in 1937, on a matter not related to his official duties, and with his removal from the scene, enthusiasm for trolleybuses waned in the corridors of the DRTT. The number of vehicles ordered proved to be in excess of requirements and three (nos.19, 24 and 26) were stored in Randwick workshops from 1937 until 1939. Despite the brave words of the GEC advertisement, there were no further conversions. The five spare vehicles, plus those which became Adelaide MTT nos.431-435 would have been sufficient to have allowed the conversion of the isolated Rockdale-Brighton-le-Sands electric tramway.

The public appreciated the new service and patronage increased greatly over the steam trams. In their last three years of operation, these had carried between 2.41 million and 2.54 million passengers annually. In their first year of operation, to 30 June 1938, the trolleybuses carried 3.69 million passengers, with a very slight increase to 3.70 million in the following year. While they did run about 25%-27% more miles than the trams and additionally served Rockdale station, the increase in passengers clearly far exceeded the numbers to be expected from this. Nor was there a corresponding increase in railway passengers from Kogarah or

The era of frozen foods has arrived and that of the trolleybus is about to close, as seen in this 1959 view of no.12 negotiating the Sans Souci loop. (V. Solomons)

Rockdale stations in this period. Clearly the increase in passenger numbers was mainly due to the attraction of the new trolleybuses to local passengers. During the war years, the internal lights were shaded with masks on the trolleybuses, as they were on trams and motorbuses serving areas which were visible from the sea.

In February 1952 no.24 emerged from Randwick workshops after a very substantial overhaul, almost amounting to a rebuilding. Diagonal bracing was applied to the front and rear windows on both sides of the lower saloon and this greatly strengthened the bodies, weakened over the years by pounding over badly-made roads – the tram tracks were not lifted until after 1947. The half-drop windows were replaced by full-depth windows sliding horizontally, those on the near side of the upper deck being limited to an opening of three inches, because of the number of trees lining the route. These alterations improved the appearance of the already handsome trolleybus. Apart from no.10, which was latterly used as a source of spare parts, all the remainder of the Kogarah fleet was similarly treated between 1952 and 1954.

From the mid-1950s onwards, what was now the Department of Government Transport (DGT) began a programme of tramway conversion and it was clear that the trolleybus system was also threatened. Surrounded by hundreds of motorbuses, 25 trolleybuses did not stand much chance of survival in the long term. At first it seemed that they would be retained until after the last tram had run. However, the service ran for the last time on 29 August 1959, no.14 operating the last journey and reaching the depot in the early hours of 30 August. Motorbuses took over on that day. Nos.6-9, 11-23 and 25/6 were towed to Manly on the north side of Sydney harbour and the dealer who bought them, a Mr R. Lougie, had plans to convert the chassis for use as diesel lorries, with the upper decks being offered for use as caravans, but this did not come to fruition. Most of the vehicles were scrapped but several were sold for further use as garden sheds. No.10, had already been withdrawn in 1957 and no.24, which was at Randwick for rebuilding when the abandonment decision was announced, was sold to an unknown purchaser for £200.

Among those which had become sheds was no.19, which in 1977 was located at Catherine Field in the city's south-west suburbs. Members of the local preservation society, the Southern Pacific Electric Railway, had been hoping to preserve a trolleybus and acquired what was by this date a body shell. Mounted on the chassis of a former AEC Regal bus, it was towed to the-then museum site at Loftus. In 1980 it was taken to the railway workshops at Chullora, where it was to be restored by apprentices of the State Rail Authority training college. Further searches had revealed the existence of two other top decks, of which that from no.21 was in excellent condition. This was taken to Chullora and mounted on to the lower deck of no.19. Electrical equipment was obtained from Hobart and Launceston and the motor was placed on mountings obtained from Johannesburg. This operator also supplied a workshop instruction manual. Air compressors were obtained from Cardiff and pedals from New Zealand. Restoration of no.19 was an international effort! The seats fitted came from a Melbourne motorbus. Restoration to running order was finally completed in 1989 and to-day no.19 can be admired at the SPER tram museum at Loftus, a fitting reminder of the Sydney trolleybus. Single-

decker no.1 has also been preserved by the Power House Museum in the city.

Sydney's trolleybuses did not carry registration plates, as they did not require to be registered under motor traffic legislation. They were painted in the new colour scheme adopted for the trams in 1933. This was an attractive combination of light green body panels, cream window surrounds and a light grey roof. Nos.3-5 had black bands below and above the lower deck windows and below those of the upper deck. As delivered the three-axle trolleybuses had a single, wide black band below the lower deck windows. The first rebuilds had a similar band below the upper deck windows, but in 1953 the arrangement was changed to one of three narrow black bands above and below the cream paint of the lower deck and below the upper deck windows. No.5 also received this paint scheme when rebuilt in 1953. From December 1954 onwards, a limited amount of advertising was carried on the 'tween deck panels and also, on some vehicles, on the waist panels.

Total number of double-deckers operated: 24

Bibliography

The Sydney Trolley Buses. Ian Mac Cowan. Published by the author, Oakleigh, 1988

Destination Paradise. R. T. Wheaton. Australian Electric Traction Association, Sydney, 1975

The Tramway Museum, St. Kilda, SA. Australian Electric Transport Museum (Inc), Adelaide, 1982

The Australian Double Decker. G. J. Travers. Historic Commercial Vehicle Association Co-operative Ltd., Sydney, 1977

From City to Suburb – a Fifty Year Journey. (The Story of NSW Government Buses). G. Travers. Sydney Tramway Museum and Historic Vehicle Association Co-op Ltd, Sydney, 1982

New South Wales Tramcar Handbook, Part Two. N. Chinn and K. McCarthy. South Pacific Electric Railway Co-operative Society Ltd., Sutherland, NSW, 1976

Electric Traction. December 1963, January and February 1964. (Adelaide history)

Trolley Buses in Hobart. Efftech Pty Ltd, Doncaster Heights, Victoria, 2002. (This video covers all Australian trolleybus systems)

The operation of double-deckers in Australia certainly showed some interesting features. Like Johannesburg, the MTT in Adelaide seems at first to have seen the trolleybus as complementary to its tram system, which continued to expand until 1944. Only latterly were the trolleybuses viewed as potential replacements for the trams, and then only to a limited extent. The use of double-deck trolleybuses to replace steam trams was a unique feature of Sydney's transport scene. But in each case the number of trolleybuses, relative first to the number of trams (Sydney had 1,502 trams in 1936), then later to that of motorbuses, was too small to ensure long-term viability. Those Australian systems which did use the trolleybus as a replacement for a tramway network – Perth, Launceston and Hobart – all opted for the single-decker.

ASIA

MALAYA

GEORGETOWN

No.20 passes the war memorial at the junction of Penang Hill Road and Ayer Itam Road, outward bound to the latter destination. (Author's collection)

The only double-decker trolleybuses to have run in mainland Asia were to be found in Georgetown, the capital of the Malayan state of Penang. This undertaking, which was owned by the municipality, traded as George Town Municipal Transport, and was in many respects a very British system. However, its trolleybus system, which was started as early as 1925, had until the mid-1950s used only single-deckers, including some extremely tiny examples, which must have been the smallest trolleybuses to run anywhere. Pre-war vehicles were Ransomes, post-war deliveries favoured Sunbeams.

As an economical way of evaluating the practicality of the double-decker, in which there was then some interest in Malaya, it was decided to import some second-hand vehicles. Even though two conductors would have to be employed, it seemed from experience in Kuala Lumpur that the extra revenue gained by the use of double-deckers more than paid for the second man's wages. Having taken this advice, GTMT then purchased five redundant C1 class AEC664T trolleybuses from London Transport, in whose fleet they were nos.138/142/148/175 and 183. All had English Electric 406A1 motors and equipment and all had identical bodywork seating 70, that on 138 being by Weymann and on the others by Metro-Cammell. The trolleybuses were shipped from London in May and June 1956 and on arrival were towed to the depot for modification. Apart from the replacement of some fixed windows at the rear of the lower saloon by horizontally-sliding panes of glass and the recovering of the seats with a plastic material – the moquette was thought to encourage cockroaches – the vehicles were very little altered in their new home. The destination box was retained but the number aperture was plated over. They were painted in a cream livery with a red band below the lower saloon windows and red between the upper and lower decks. The trolleybuses were renumbered in George Town, becoming nos.20-24, these being ex LT nos.142/148/175/183 and 138 respectively.

Thus altered, the double-deckers were placed in service on the Jelutong route. Unfortunately they could not negotiate the turning circle at the city end of the route at Weld Quay and this had to be enlarged, at considerable expense. In some places the overhead had to be raised to allow them to operate safely. They did not work on any other route. The post of lower deck conductor was considered to be senior and its holder was responsible for replacing dewired trolley booms and operating frogs at junctions. Although popular with passengers and crews, they were not a great success in Malaya and all were withdrawn from service on 13 November 1959. No further double-deckers were bought and the entire system closed in one operation in July 1961. Although unsuccessful attempts were made to sell the newest single-deckers, the Londoners were broken up immediately afterward by George Cohen (Far East) Ltd. The experiment of using double-deckers was deemed to have been a failure.

Total number of double-deckers operated: 5

Bibliography

Bus Journeys through Malaya in the 1950s. F.W. York. DTS Publishing, Croydon, 2001
Buses Illustrated no.34, November-December 1957, nos.73 & 74, April & May 1961
London Trolleybuses Abroad. The Omnibus Society and the PSV Circle, publication no.LTB1, 1965

A book on this system is in course of preparation by DTS Publishing, Croydon and another by an Australian author.

SRI LANKA

COLOMBO

During the second world war, in 1944, the City Council of Colombo purchased the somewhat antiquated tramway system from the private company which had operated it since its opening in 1898, and there was mention of a possible replacement by trolleybuses in about ten years' time. In 1950 the decision was taken to proceed with the first part of this plan and 20 BUT 9611T trolleybuses were ordered through John Pook and Company, the purchasing agents for the municipality in Britain. These were 26ft long and 7ft 6in wide, being fitted with Weymann 56-seat (30/26) bodies.

Followed by a fine specimen of a pre-war Austin car and a post-war Ford Prefect, no.9 negotiates a roundabout. Both vehicles have just overtaken a bullock cart. (F.W. York, courtesy Ian Allan library)

English Electric equipment was specified, with 120hp motors, automatic acceleration and series-dynamic SD control system. That company was obviously rather proud of these vehicles and they featured in its advertisements for some years. Although stated to have been built to meet the requirements of the General Manager, R. Cangarayar, the buses would have looked at home on any British municipal system and were in fact designed to meet British MOT requirements. All side windows in the lower saloon and five in the upper saloon were of half-drop opening design, as were the two windows at the front of the upper deck, and photographs generally show these open to the full. Drivers

A profile of no.20. (F.W. York)

No.16 arrives at a busy Fort terminus. (F.W. York)

normally kept the upper half of the windscreen open also. Six extractor ventilators were fitted in the roof, with an air intake in the front dome panelling, and the lower saloon was ventilated by an air intake above the driver's cab, from which fresh air was conveyed to the saloon by a trunking system. The cab itself had two scoop ventilators. Apart from this, however, there were no concessions to local climatic conditions. Large destination and separate number boxes were fitted front and rear, to allow display of the destination and intermediate points in English, Sinhalese and Tamil. Comfortable leather seats were provided in both saloons and, with shaded light fittings, the trolleybuses offered a far higher standard of comfort than the trams they replaced and, in their green and cream livery, with gold numerals, looked very attractive. The green was of a medium shade, akin to that used in England by Exeter Corporation. Fleet numbers were 1-20 and the trolleybuses carried British-style registration plates. This series was registered CV2237-2256, almost but not quite in order as no.20 was CV2248, a registration which should have been given to no.12.

To house the trolleybuses, a new depot was built in Bloemendahl Street, off the route of the first service where it branched from the Grand Pass tram line, some distance from the tram depot in Gasworks Street. A Guy Vixen tower wagon was acquired.

The first trolleybus to be completed was tested on the London Transport system between Hampton Court and Fulwell in April 1951 and gave every satisfaction. The completed vehicles were then exported to Colombo but their entry into service was considerably delayed due to a dispute between the municipality and the nationalised electricity undertaking, concerning the removal of certain standards which had formerly supported the tramway overhead. This was finally settled in July 1952 and service began on 22 July 1953 on what became service 3, from Fort to Kotahena via

Marandana. This was a replacement of the tramway along Armour Street and an extension, not previously served by trams. A further 15 similar vehicles, also 56-seaters but with bodywork by East Lancashire Coachbuilders, nos.21-35, were ordered in 1953 and delivered between April and June 1954. They were registered irregularly between CV4199 and CV4259. Once again the interior fittings represented the best of what was by 1954 former British practice, with comfortable leather upholstered seats, shaded light fittings and polished timber trim to the window surrounds and ventilators. The arrival of these new vehicles in 1954 allowed two new services to be inaugurated on 7 July of that year, from Fort to Borella via Marandana, service 1, and an inter-suburban working from Borella to Kotahena, service 4. The trolleybuses were hailed as a great success and it was decided to proceed with the tramway conversion. An extension was made to the system on 17 July 1957, when service 2 from Fort to Madampitiya via Barber Street was begun. This was a replacement for and extension of the Grand Pass tram line.

The double-deckers seem to have fallen from favour and for this service 26 Sunbeam MF2B single-deckers were ordered in 1956, nos.36-61. These were of two lengths, the last six being 35ft long, with seats for 34 passengers, while nos.36-55 were 30ft long and seated 26. A new system of registration had now been adopted and these trolleybuses were numbered in the 33 series. The shorter vehicles were numbered variously between 33.720 and 33.791, while their longer counterparts were between 33.193 and 33.379. All were fitted with dual door (front and rear) bodies by East Lancashire, having standee windows. In many respects they resembled the single-deckers built by the same firm in 1952 for Glasgow Corporation, although these had the exit door behind the front axle. The longer vehicles had six side windows, the shorter ones five. The conductor had a desk on the offside at the rear and passenger flow was from rear to

No.25 in the city centre, one of the batch with East Lancs bodies. (F.W. York)

front. By this time, polished timber fittings had given way to plastic laminates, but these trolleybuses were still turned out to a very high standard. It was an advanced design for the period and, when one of the 30ft vehicles was tested under the wires of the South Lancashire Transport network, it must have made the latter's veteran double-deckers vehicles look even more antique. These operated all workings on service 2 and supplemented the double-deckers elsewhere as required. It was now stated that single-deckers were better suited to local conditions. Average speed was given as 10mph and a two-minute headway was operated, presumably in peak hours. Unlike the trams, which were by this time somewhat run-down, the trolleybuses were kept in pristine condition. The last 2½ miles of tramway, which are thought to have been the Borella line as far as Marandana, was abandoned on 30 June 1960.

By 1963 frequencies were 6 minutes off-peak and 4 minutes at peak times. Ultimate-type ticket machines were used and each service was divided into three sections, fares being 5 cents, 10 cents and 15 cents for one, two or three sections. At that time 5 cents was almost equal to 1d.

In the same year as the single-deckers arrived, the Ceylon Transport Board was formed and began to acquire all the bus operations in the country. This probably explains the renumbering of the trolleybus services in the 166x series. The creation of the CTB seems to have spelled doom for the almost-new trolleybus system. Exactly what happened is not clear, but it seems that the municipality, seeing little future in transport, wanted to sell the undertaking to the CTB and the latter had no desire to maintain a fleet of 61 trolleybuses among hundreds of diesel buses. Early in 1964 many trolleybuses were damaged during a strike. Some kind of agreement with the CTB must have been reached, since the last trolleybuses ran on 1 December of that year, being replaced by CTB motorbuses. Ironically many of the replacing buses were ex-London transport RTL double-deckers. Some of the single-deckers were later used as

trailers behind single-deck Skoda motorbuses but no use or buyer was found for the double-deckers, which were observed derelict in a field in 1972. Perhaps they are still there!

At some point, probably after the CTB was formed, the services were renumbered. Service 1 became 1667, service 3 became 1669 but the order of renumbering of the other two services is not known.

It was a sad end to an interesting experiment. Colombo was in the event to be the last British-type trolleybus system to be opened anywhere and, apart from the tri-lingual destination information, the trolleybuses would have looked quite at home had they suddenly been air-lifted to Nottingham. It was a bold experiment to implant an operation of this kind in a city in a tropical climate, in a developing country, several thousand miles from the others. It must also have cost a great deal of money, which the newly-independent country could ill afford, and much of this was subsequently wasted. In the end, the new trolleybus system failed, not through any fault of its own but through the working of local and national politics.

Total number of double-deckers operated: 35

Bibliography

Modern Transport, 5 May 1951
Buses Annual 1964, Ian Allan Ltd, London
Website of Hans Bjorkman, Sweden

THAILAND

BANGKOK

There may have been an enquiry from Bangkok about purchase of 16 London Q1s. As Thailand drives on the left, such a purchase would have made sense if the authorities in the capital had been considering trolleybuses. Whatever the truth, the matter was not pursued and trolleybuses have not at any time run in Bangkok.

Bibliography

Buses Worldwide, various issues 1999-2002
The London Trolleybus. M.J. Dryhurst. Dryhurst Publications, London, 1961

HONG KONG

In 1999 the Hong Kong operator Citybus obtained permission to equip a demonstration line for trolleybuses. After some consideration of bringing from Britain the Dennis Dominator demonstrator built for South Yorkshire in 1984 (now at Sandtoft museum), work began in the following year on converting bus no.701 to a trolleybus. This bus was a 10.3m three axle Dennis Dragon and was fitted with an electric motor and trolley booms. It was already air-conditioned and the conversion made it the world's first air-conditioned double-deck trolleybus. The project team was headed by the company's engineering consultant, John Blay. This was something of an international effort, since parts came from Britain, France, Denmark, Italy and Switzerland. The company considered the experiment to be a demonstration of its social responsibility, in helping to combat pollution on Hong Kong's streets. The launch of the project coincided with the Better Air Quality conference, held in Hong Kong in September 2000, at which John Blay was a speaker.

By early 2001 no.701 had, after considerable delay, also received an auxiliary diesel power unit and had been tested on a track at Wong Chuk Hang parking site, Ocean Park, where a short length of overhead had been erected by a team from Beijing. As there were only 18 traction poles erected for the overhead, it may be debated whether such a short line would adequately replicate service conditions, but it was the intention to run the trolleybus along it intensively.

The vehicle was repainted green to emphasise its environmentally-friendly credentials and the seats were also re-upholstered in green anti-vandal material. It did not operate in public service, although passengers were from time to time carried on the test runs, no fare being charged. These tests took place in the first half of 2001 and since then little has been heard of the experiment. Consideration was given to the possibility of moving no.701 to Wellington, where the trolleybus system is operated by Stagecoach, at that time the parent company of Citybus, but on closer investigation, it appeared that it was too high to fit under Wellington's overhead and the plan was dropped.

Bibliography

Buses Worldwide, various issues 2000-2002
Citybus web site news, 2000

Five-window 1956-1965 Colombo 36-55 Sunbeam MF2B/EE/East Lancashire B26D.

Six-window 1956-1965 Colombo 56-61 Sunbeam MF2B/EE/East Lancashire B34D.

Drawings by David Jones.

EUROPE

RUSSIA

The imported AEC double-decker in service on Leningradskoe Shosse. (Alexander Sharin and Roland Box)

MOSCOW

Trolleybus operation in this city and in the USSR began on 5 November 1933, when two single-deckers built on lorry chassis were tried on the Leningradskoe Shosse (Leningrad Highway). These trials were successful and public operation began on 15 November. Services were soon expanded and trolleybus systems were installed in other cities. All vehicles used were single-deckers.

In 1937 construction began of a permanent exhibition of the achievements of Soviet agriculture (VSKHV) on a site in the northern part of the city. To link this with the city centre, a special trolleybus route was constructed, operated as line 2K.

As all public transport in Moscow was more or less permanently overcrowded, the then head of the city's Bolshevik Party Committee, Nikita Kruschev, suggested that a trial should be made of British-type double-deckers and in November 1936 an AEC 664T, with English Electric

A rear view of 1007 at Sovetskaya Square in the late 1940s. (Alexander Sharin)

A rear view of the AEC single-decker in service on Gorky Street in 1947. (Alexander Sharin)

equipment, was ordered. On 6 April 1937 the completed trolleybus left Britain for Leningrad (St. Petersburg) on board SS *Luga*. From there it was towed to Kalinin (Tver) and was there loaded on to a barge to be taken along the River Volga to

One of the Russian-built double-deckers in Gorky Street in Moscow. (Alexander Sharin)

Severnyi, Moscow's northern river port, which it reached on 6 July. Trials began from no.2 depot on 22 July and the trolleybus entered service on line 1 on 1 September. To allow it to operate, the overhead along Leningradskoye Shosse had to be raised to a height of 5.8m/19ft 4in and as this work was not quite complete, the trolleybus was at first confined to the section between Byelorusskiy voksal and Koptev. By 11 September, it was able to traverse the entire length of the line. It proved to be successful in operation. One AEC 664T single-decker was also acquired.

Following this experiment and using the AEC as a prototype, it was decided to order eleven similar trolleybuses from the Jaroslavl factory, which had been given the task of building the nation's trolleybuses. The first began test running on 26 June 1938 and entered passenger service on 13 September. Others arrived in the first half of 1939 and the final vehicle reached Moscow on 14 October of that year. They were classified Jatb-3 and were numbered 1001-1011. Seating capacity was 40/32 and standing capacity was probably infinite. As the bodies were 8ft wide and the chassis of the AEC had been designed for bodies six inches narrower, there was a pronounced overhang over the side members. As the buses had been built to run alongside single-deckers, they were only 4.4m high and this did not allow adequate headroom for standees. Two conductors were carried, one for each deck and there was a single rear platform, fitted with folding doors. There appears to have been a single seat on the platform, but whether this was for the conductor is not clear. As with all Russian trolleybuses, livery was blue; the AEC had white bands in typically British style. Internally the Jatb-3 trolleybuses were finished to quite a high standard, with comfortable upholstered seats. They had rather less ornamentation than contemporary British buses, but in every other respect were fully comparable.

In 1939 the overhead on the section of line 2K between Ploshchad Sverdlova and Rzhevskiy voksal was raised to

A frame diagram of a Jatb-3 trolleybus. (Alexander Sharin)

5.6m height to allow double-deckers to run on this line, which they did from 13 March. However, on 10 April of that year, lines 1 and 2k were combined to form a new double-

A view of the AEC passing the former entrance to the VSKHV exhibition of in the autumn of 1939. (Anatoly Egerov)

A Jatb-3 at the same location, also in 1939. (Anatoly Egerov)

deck service 12, running from Koptevo to Rzhevskiy voksal. The double-deckers were then concentrated in no.1 depot. All survived the war, during which they were worked extremely hard, and in the period 1945-47 the bodies were strengthened, apart from that on one which was withdrawn in 1946. It was probably at this period that they were given an additional front door. Given the loads carried during the war years, these problems with wooden-framed bodies were no disgrace to the builders. The others were withdrawn between 1948 and 1953, when the last three were taken out of service. The AEC was withdrawn in 1948. One survived until the late 1950s, as a store at the Fourth Depot.

There have been reports that Leyland TB3 chassis were

A view of the lower saloon of one of the Russian built vehicles, after the fitting of a front door. (Alexander Sharin)

A view of the upper deck. (Alexander Sharin)

A still from a 1947 film showing one of the Jatb-3 trolleybuses on the Tverskoy bridge near the Bylorussia station. (Alexander Sharin)

exported to Moscow in 1938 and that BUT chassis went to the same destination in 1948. It has not been possible to confirm any of these.

The double-deckers were reasonably successful, but no more double-deckers were built and it has been rumoured that Stalin was not in favour of the type, on the grounds that it was liable to overturn. On the other hand, Mr Kruschev's enthusiasm for double-deckers must have become well-known, since in 1958 he was presented with a post-war Berlin double-deck motorbus, which for some years operated sightseeing tours in Moscow. There is a model of a double-decker, together with those of all other classes of trolleybus which have run in Moscow, in a small museum in Fili depot. Details: Length 9.47m/31ft Width 2.4m/8ft Weight 8,500kg/8tons, 7cwt.

Total number of double-deckers operated: 12

Bibliography

Trolleybus Magazine nos.194, 196 and 234, March/April and July/August 1994 and November/December 2000

PORTUGAL

PORTO

Transport in this city is operated by the Serviço de Transportes Colectivos do Porto (STCP). Trolleybus operation began as tramway replacement on 3 May 1959 with

At the end of a morning rush hour in April 1972, no.137 descends the steep hill leading down from Carmo to Praça de Liberedade. It is followed by one of Porto's trams, which were later barred from this hill after two accidents. (Author)

No.119 and another double-decker at Bolhao in the city centre in August 1970. (Author)

20 BUT LETB1 single-deckers. These had UTIC bodies built in Portugal, under licence from Park Royal. A further six were acquired in 1964, these having three doors instead of two and consequently reduced seating capacity.

The fleet was greatly expanded in 1968 by the purchase of 75 Italian Lancia trolleybuses, mounted on the firm's 120/003 chassis. To house this expanded fleet, a new depot was opened at Areosa. Fifty were double-deckers, nos.101-150, with electrical equipment by CGE of Italy and regenerative braking. Bodywork for both types was by the Portugese firm of Dalfa, that for the double-deckers being based closely on that fitted to the second batch of Leyland Atlanteans

No.117 approaching Campanha station in August 1970. (Author)

Repainted in the later orange and cream livery is no.121 in Rua Bonfim, 7 June 1992. (Peter Haseldine)

supplied to Porto. However, unlike the Atlanteans, the trolleybuses had a high floor level, necessitating two steps at each doorway. Both entrance and exit were enclosed by power-operated folding doors. Seating was 43/25 and the official standing capacity was 15. A conductor's post was provided over the nearside wheel arch and two rear-ascending staircases and two doors allowed passenger flow from rear to front. In practice, most conductors seemed to prefer to collect fares in the traditional manner and passenger flow was not really enforced in Porto. The interior was finished to a high standard, with fluorescent lighting, and deep cushions made the red leather seats, on both decks, unusually comfortable. Trolley retrievers were fitted. The original and very attractive livery was one of deep red body panels, cream window surrounds and a grey roof. This was from 1982 changed to one of orange and off-white with a grey roof. This change did nothing for the appearance of the trolleybuses. The opening windows at the front of the upper deck were replaced by fixed panes.

This was the last production batch of double-deck trolleybuses to enter service anywhere. They were used mainly on services 11 and 12, to São Pedro da Cova and Gondomar respectivley, from the inauguration of trolleybus service on these on 17 November 1968. These ran quite far out into the countryside to the east of the city, over sometimes indifferent road surfaces, but the double-deckers performed well and frequently carried capacity loads. In 1990 they were converted for one-person operation, using the front door as entrance and the rear as exit, but they did not run in this condition for very long, since they were withdrawn with the closure of services 11, 12 and 14 on 4 March 1995. This date therefore marked the end of commercial operation of double-deck trolleybuses. The last remnants of the system closed on 29 December 1997. It was stated that the operator intended to resume service at a later date, with single-deckers only, but to date this has not occurred. However, no.140 was gifted to the

Lower saloon, looking towards, the rear, showing the capacious platform. (Author)

Upper saloon, looking forwards. (Author)

buses were used in the 1920s and by 1925 the Compãnia General de Autobuses had 64 of these. The first examples were imported complete, but those placed in service in 1929 had bodies built by the Tranvias de Barcelona in its own workshops. These had enclosed upper decks and were of an advanced design for the time. They were constructed on Tilling-Stevens TS4X chassis, which were acquired in 1928 from the Compãnia de Autobuses de Madrid SA. The reason for using second-hand chassis was that an international exhibition was to be held in Barcelona in 1929 and it was thought that there would be insufficient buses to cope with the traffic resulting from this. They had petrol-electric transmission, with a 100V motor and originally ran on semi-pneumatic tyres. As motorbuses they were 8m long, 2.3m wide and 4.25m high. Seating was for 64 passengers. Curiously the new buses were not numbered consecutively but as follows: 201-210, 212/3, 220-222, 224-244. The design was known as the España class. Twenty-five were actually built in 1929 and a further 11 in 1930. In the 1930s a further 32 buses were built, to two slightly different designs and these consisted of 261/2 and 275-310. The first batch then became known as the 200 class. The main improvement was that the upper deck was extended to a point about half way over the engine, increasing the seating capacity by four and also giving a more balanced profile.

The undertaking suffered severely during the civil war and some vehicles were destroyed.

Immediately after the conclusion of hostilities, it was decided to inaugurate trolleybus services in Barcelona, the first use of these in Spain. As it was by then impossible to buy new vehicles abroad, even if the money could have been found, twenty of the España class of buses were rebuilt as trolleybuses. To carry out this work and also build new bodies

Sandtoft Museum in England in 1996 and is now preserved there in operating condition, still carrying its orange and white livery. Sister bus no.102 is preserved by STCP in Porto, having been restored to original livery.

> **Total number of double-deckers operated: 50**

Bibliography

The Tramways of Portugal (4th edition). B. R. King and J. H. Price. Light Rail Transit Association, London, 1995

SPAIN

BARCELONA

The capital of Catalonia has a long tradition of operating double-deckers. Double-deck Tilling-Stevens petrol-electric

No. 513 on Paralelo, 14 June 1957. (Ray De Groote)

A contrast in styling between trolleybus no.514 and a semi-PCC tram, April 1958. (Pam Eaton)

for trams and buses, TB set up a subsidiary company, Maquinaria & Elementos de Transporte, generally know as Maquitrans. A new driving cab was fitted in a central position, where the engine had been, and a plain bonnet with twin headlights replaced the radiator. The bodies were completely overhauled, but were not altered in any other way. All but one came from the 275 class, as follows: 276/8, some from nos.280-287 and others from nos.290-304. At some date after 1945, no.204 of the first group was also converted. The trolleybuses took the numbers 501-520 and with them services were inaugurated on 7 October 1941. Given the economic conditions prevailing in Spain at the time, this development reflected great credit on all concerned, not least the works staff who had managed to rebuild the vehicles. The line was a great success and was soon extended. A second service began in 1943 and others followed in 1948-50.

No.522, seen on Paralelo on 14 June 1957, is one of the later series, but as can be seen, these were identical to the earlier version. (Ray De Groote)

BUT no.622 Easter 1958. (Pam Eaton)

No.626 out of service at Tetuan terminus. (B. A. Jenkins)

Maquitrans built some single-deckers for these, but for additional services to be opened in 1950-53, it was decided to have more double-deckers. These were built new, possibly incorporating some parts for motorbuses and were to the same design as the 1940 vehicles, and as these basically dated from 1929, the new buses, nos.521-538, looked somewhat antiquated. Nevertheless, they seem to have performed satisfactorily.

They soon looked even more old-fashioned, since an order was placed with BUT in Britain for 27 9651T three-axle chassis. Maquitrans fitted motors and control equipment and a local firm built double-deck bodies of modern appearance, fully comparable with British trolleybuses of the early 1950s. They were built for passenger flow from rear to front, the platforms being enclosed by power-operated folding doors. There was a conductor's post on the nearside, just above the

A rear view of the old and the new, with a double-deck tram coming in on the right. (Pam Eaton)

No.519 is seen in August 1964, at Tirquin Gonar (Peter Haseldine)

rear axle, and a central spiral staircase was provided. Fleet numbers were 601-627.

Unfortunately in the early 1960s official opinion swung away from electric street traction and also from double-deckers. The older double-deckers were gradually withdrawn, about twelve remaining in service in 1964, while the BUTs were rebuilt as single-deckers in 1963. When the Barcelona system finally closed in 1968, these were sold to Valencia. Some were further sold to Pontevedra when the Valencia system closed and there they ran alongside ex-LT Q1s. No.610 is now preserved in the Catalan Museum of Transport.

Livery of all types of vehicles in Barcelona was red and cream. On the 500 class trolleybuses, there were cream window surrounds on both decks and a cream roof, but the BUTs had a much more traditionally British style of livery, with three cream bands and a red roof. Full depth horizontally sliding windows were fitted in both saloons of all trolleybuses.

> **Total number of double-deckers operated: 65**

CADIZ

This undertaking, the Tranvia de Cádiz a San Fernando, operated a tram service between the two places of its title. In 1951 the line was equipped for trolleybuses and four BUT double-deckers, numbered 1 to 4, were acquired to run an

A commercial postcard showing no.1 and part of another of the double-deckers on Avenida Ramon de Carranza (Peter Haseldine collection)

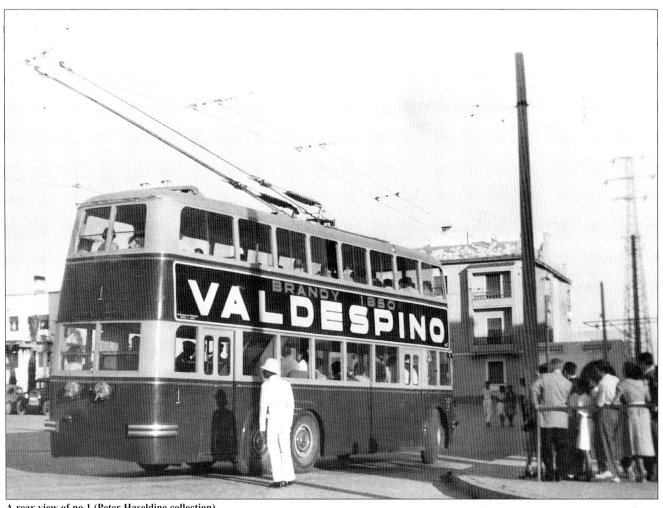

A rear view of no.1 (Peter Haseldine collection)

express service, trams continuing to provide a local service. The bodies, which seated 73, were by the Spanish firm of Carde and Escoriaza of Zaragoza, a firm which built many railway carriages and trams, but very few trolleybuses. The undertaking was part of a group which included this firm, as well as the transport undertaking of Tolosa and Zaragoza. Livery was dark green with yellow lining, silver window surrounds and silver roof. There were rear and forward doors and a single staircase was fitted just ahead of the rear door on the nearside. The double-deckers lasted until 1966 but the exact date of closure of the system is not known.

Total number of double-deckers operated: 4

In May 1960 London Transport announced that it was prepared to sell the Q1 trolleybuses delivered in 1948 and 1952 and a number of foreign operators expressed interest. Finally in February 1961 it was confirmed that 88 of these vehicles would go to six Spanish operators. Three others – Tarragona-Reus, Vigo and Zaragoza – obtained 37 trolley-buses of the remainder of the Q1 class of 127 vehicles later in the year, leaving two which were retained in Britain for preservation. The sale of these trolleybuses allowed London Transport to complete its conversion scheme in 1962.

BILBAO

Transport in the Basque city was in the 1960s operated by Transportes Urbanos del Gran Bilbao SA, a municipal under-taking. Trolleybus operation had begun just after that in Barcelona, in 1940.

This operator bought 25 of the London Transport Q1 class in 1961, these being the odd-numbered vehicles of the 1952 delivery, nos.1843-1891. These were renumbered by the simple expedient of dropping the initial 1 and so took the odd numbers between 843 and 891. Not all were immediately used, the last entering service in 1967. They were quite heavily rebuilt for service in Bilbao. The new rear platform was enclosed with automatic folding doors. A conductor's desk, a central spiral staircase and a front exit, with folding doors, were fitted in the lower saloon, in which seating capacity was reduced to 8, these being single seats on old frames, located over the wheel arches. Some extra seats were squeezed into the upper saloon and seating capacity was therefore 43/8. The buses were initially painted all over red but were later given cream window surrounds. They were used on five of the trolleybus services, lines 2, 5, 6, 8 and 10. The road surfaces in the city were then not in good condition and standards of maintenance were low. As a result, the bodywork of the Q1s tended to become loose and by 1970 they were in poor condition. The last ran in 1977 and trolleybus services were abandoned in the next year.

The undertaking also made use of double-deck motor-buses and two of the Q1s, nos. 877 and 887 were rebuilt as motorbuses, taking the numbers 277 and 287. The chassis was lengthened by five feet, a diesel engine fitted and a forward exit, with a two-section folding door, provided. In this condition they seated 67 passengers, but could carry over 100 with standees. It had been intended to rebuild eight in all, but as the two so treated were not considered to have been a complete success, no more were altered.

Total number of double-deckers operated: 23

A CORUÑA

Tranvias de la Coruña replaced some of its trams by trolley-buses in 1948, these being French and Spanish single-

No.859 at Puente de la Victoria, 5 June 1965. (Ray De Groote)

No.33 (LT no.1817) at Puerta Real in September 1968. (Peter Haseldine)

deckers. To complete the programme, 25 Q1 trolleybuses were acquired from London Transport, of which 12 were placed in service in 1962 to replace the last trams. These were numbered 23-34. The remainder were numbered 35-47 and were stored for some years until required. Ultimately six of the stored vehicles, nos.38/40/43/45/46 and 47, plus one which had been in service, were cut down to single-deck form. Three further Q1s were bought from Pontevedra in 1964 and numbered 48-50, the last of these also becoming a single-decker.

Eleven services in all were operated but the double-deckers were normally confined to services 1, 2 and 3. On 7 July 1964 no.36 carried members of the Tramway Museum Society on a special tour of the system. The first few to enter service simply had the platforms and stairs reversed, but all the acquisitions were rebuilt with front exit, folding doors enclosing both platforms, a straight, rearward-ascending staircase over the nearside rear axle and large bumpers. A desk was provided for the conductor and, at a later date, turnstiles were fitted at the entrance to the lower saloon, which then seated only 16 or 19 passengers (sources give both figures). The upper deck continued to accommodate 36. Livery was blue and cream with a maroon roof. The front roof dome was cream. As the London moquette wore out, shaped plywood seats were fitted. Although maintenance was good, the condition of local roads caused the bodies to deteriorate and latterly the buses ran with marked vibration. These were, by a very short margin, the last of the Q1s to survive in Spain and final day of operation of the type was 4 January 1979.

Total number of double-deckers operated: 23

A CORUÑA-CARBALLO

This unusual radial line, with a length of 33km/20.5 miles, was built as a trolleybus line by the Copmaña de Trolebuses

The hilly terrain served by this undertaking is well shown in this view of no.24 (LT no.1774) approaching the summit between A Coruña and Arteijo, in the early evening of 3 September 1968. (Peter Haseldine)

No.21 (LTno.1772) manoeuvres with the help of a T-pole outside the depot at Arteijo on 3 September 1968. (Peter Haseldine)

Coruña-Carballo and opened in 1950 using German equipment, which had first been ordered in 1943. A goods service was provided, using trailers. Eight Q1s were bought initially, the provisional allocation being LT nos.1766/67/69, 1770/727/73 and 1774. Only seven were actually used in service, as nos.20-26, these being in order ex-LT nos.1770/72/66/69/74/76 and 1773. The eighth, which had been LT 1771, remained in the depot as a source of spare

One of the Pontevedra trolleybuses given a front staircase, no.105 (LT no.1801) passes Pastora en route to Marin on 30 August 1968. (Peter Haseldine)

No.103 (LT no.1811) clearly shows its open rear platform as it leaves Marin on 6 September 1972. (Peter Haseldine)

parts. A further example was acquired in 1969 from Vigo. The rear platforms were altered to suit right-hand traffic and given manually-operated outward-opening doors. No other changes were made to the design and seating remained as in London. Fares, which were quite high by contemporary Spanish standards, were collected by a roving conductor. The double-deckers were used to supplement the basic service at busy periods and to provide short workings. They did not tow the goods trailers. Livery was silver with red bands and no advertisements were carried. The destination boxes were plated over and no indication of the service was given to prospective passengers, but probably most of these would have known the system anyway. Maintenance was not a strong point of this system and dewirements were frequent. Spare trolleyheads were kept in a small cupboard in the rear roof dome, reached by an iron ladder fitted at the rear. However, every effort was made to locate lost items and passengers often joined the crew in a session of "hunt the trolleyhead". Vehicles often ran in service without the cover of the front inspection panel. The last trolleybus ran in 1971.

Total number of double-deckers operated: 7

PONTEVEDRA

Services here and in the adjacent port of Marin were run by the Tranvia Electrico de Pontevedra SA. Services had begun in 1943, using Leyland single-deckers which had been ordered for Canton. Two services were operated.

A certain amount of confusion surrounds the purchase of the Q1s by this operator. It was intended to buy twelve Q1s and the provisional allocation was LT nos.1776/ 77/88/91/95/99, 1801/3/4, 1811/16/24. A problem of some kind then intervened and it has been suggested that, due to some confusion over import licences, a total of 24 Q1s was finally bought, most then being passed on to other operators. Only eight actually arrived in Pontevedra and of these, five saw service, numbered 101-105. No.102 was renumbered 105 in 1976, when the first bus with that number was scrapped.

The first three to enter service were not rebuilt, save for the change of the platform to allow right hand running. On these, the conductor either stood on the rear platform or sat in the stair well, collecting fares from passengers as they boarded. Nos.104/5, which entered service after 1964, were given a straight stairway at the front left hand side of the lower saloon and a conductor's desk at the rear. A new front exit was fitted and both this and the rear platform were given power-operated folding doors. All were given substantial front bumpers and over the years slatted wooden seats replaced the originals. The livery of light blue and cream was enhanced by cream wheel centres and a good deal of polished chrome. The vehicles were maintained in excellent condition and became favourites with visiting enthusiasts from Britain. They were withdrawn in December 1978. This undertaking also had six Leyland TB5 single-deckers, part of the order diverted from Canton.

It would appear that the other three vehicles were broken up, although there have been reports that one was rebuilt as a motorbus, an experiment which was unsuccessful.

Total number of double-deckers operated: 5

SAN SEBASTIAN

The municipally-owned Compania del Tranvia de San Sebastian bought the 25 even-numbered trolleybuses from the 1952 batch of Q1s, LT nos.1842-1890. The town's trams had, from 1948 onwards, been replaced by single-deck trolleybuses, including 27 BUT 9641Ts. The new arrivals took fleet numbers 71-95. They were given a smart blue and cream livery with red lining and a silver roof. They worked the four city services, replacing the original Hispano-Suiza single-deckers of 1948. Other single-deckers continued to provide service on longer radial routes. Generally the city's fleet was maintained in good condition. The first four double-

No.73 (LT no.1870) leaves the town centre for Anoeta in August 1968 (Peter Haseldine)

No.71 (LT no.1888) enters Igueldo terminus on 22 August 1968. (Peter Haseldine)

deckers initially retained the traditional stairs, though of course reversed, but were given a conductor's desk fitted inside the lower saloon, in which some seats were removed. Seating capacity was 40/20. It seems that this arrangement led to congestion at the rear of the vehicle and all the others were given a straight rearward-ascending staircase at the offside rear of the lower saloon. A front exit was added and a fixed post for the conductor was created at the front of the lower saloon. Seating was 36/22. The earlier conversions were later altered to bring them into line with these. The former number boxes at front and rear were used to house the destination indicators. All had been withdrawn by 1972.

Total number of double-deckers operated: 25

SANTANDER-ASTILLERO

This interurban line was operated by the Compania de Trolebuses Santander-Astillero, from Santander inland for eight miles, using the wires of the town system for the first part of the journey. (The town system did not use double-deckers.) It had originally been a tramway and trolleybus operation began in 1953, using German single-deckers. Before buying any of the Q1s, the manager visited Fulwell depot in London and personally chose the six vehicles which had most recently been overhauled. These became S-A nos.7/9/10/8/6/11 respectively. The depot at Maliaño, about the mid-way point of the line, had to be enlarged and the roof raised to accommodate the new arrivals. While this work was being carried out, nos.1821 and 1775 were converted in the open outside the depot in April/May 1961. The remainder were stored in Astillero, to be dealt with once work on the depot was finished.

The new livery was simply a variation on that of London Transport, with a grey waistband, grey roof and a chocolate rear roof dome. The rainshields over the saloon windows were retained from London days and the whole effect was enhanced by the total absence of advertisements, unusual for Spain. In fact, this operator became so enthusiastic about the new colour scheme that the existing fleet of MAN single-deckers, which had previously been painted grey, was similarly treated.

The stair and rear platform were of course reversed and fitted with doors and a central exit, with doors, was created in the lower saloon. Seating became 40/21. The fleet number was placed in the former number aperture at front and rear and glass plates, bearing the names of the two termini, were placed in the destination boxes. An unusual feature of operation was that at peak periods access to the upper deck was permitted only to those passengers travelling at least half the length of the line. For at least the first years of their life in Spain, these trolleybuses were well cared for and presented a smart appearance, but latterly standards declined. All the Q1s were withdrawn in late 1974, but not immediately scrapped, and the line was converted to diesel buses in 1975. In 1977 no.8 (ex LT 1812) was acquired for preservation by a group of British enthusiasts and, after some work and fitting of missing items with parts from other buses, it was found capable of running on its batteries, despite the time in store. After a somewhat hazardous journey to the coast, it returned to Britain on 19 June 1977 and is now at Sandtoft museum, having been fully restored to its original London condition.

Total number of double-deckers operated: 6

No.8 (LT no.1812) at the station of the narrow gauge railway, 3 June 1965. (Ray De Groote)

One of the two Q1s in Reus. (tramway.com collection)

T87 (LT1793) is seen leaving Tarragona on 10 September 1968. (Peter Haseldine)

TARRAGONA

A radial trolleybus line of 14km/8.75 miles was opened in 1952 between this seaport and holiday resort and the inland industrial town of Reus. The fleet was known by the initials of the company FIRTESA. The actual title was Filovas Interurbanos Reus-Tarragona y Extensiones SA, which might best be translated as "Interurban trolley line Reus-Tarragona and Extensions Ltd". (No extensions were actually built.). Two Q1s, LT nos.1792 and 1793, were acquired to supplement the single-deck fleet of French Vetras and ex-Barcelona Maquitrans, and took fleet numbers T86/7, in order. The platform was altered and folding doors were fitted, but no other changes were made and the buses continued to seat 70 passengers. Livery was bright blue and cream, the latter being attractively swept down around the indicator at the front. The front and rear destination indicators were retained, the former number aperture showing the fleet number while the destination aperture showed permanently "Tarragona-Reus y Vice-Versa". Trolleybus services ended in 1973.

Total number of double-deckers operated: 2

VIGO

With a view to replacing its trams, the Tranvias Electricos de Vigo CA acquired eleven Q1s, but in the event they were not used and most remained stored in the depot until scrapped. There seems to have been some idea of converting them to single-deckers and in 1964 a mock-up of a new rear end was built in the tramway workshops. No further work was done on these vehicles which remained in store in the workshops. Ultimately the town's trams were replaced by motorbuses and the Q1s were broken up, apart from no.1789 which passed to A Coruña. An attempt was made to purchase ex LT no.1830 and return it to Britain, but this was unsuccessful.

ZARAGOZA

The transport system in this city was operated by Tranvias de Zaragoza, and, as mentioned, this was linked with the C&E rolling stock builders. Twelve Q1s were bought, of which six were not placed in service until 1965. The first six took the numbers 51-56, the remainder 71-76. At this time, trams were still the main form of urban transport in the city and the trolleybus, which had first been introduced about 1950, played a secondary role.

All the Q1s were given a front exit and platform doors were fitted to this and the rear platform. The staircase was re-positioned to the centre of the offside of the lower saloon and a conductor's desk was fitted adjacent to the rear platform. Seating capacity was now 36/19. Livery was a very attractive silver, with green window surrounds, the green being swept down over the front dash. Latterly wooden slatted seats replaced those originally fitted. The first batch to enter service were used exclusively on the service to Cuidad Jardim (Garden City), which seems to have been something of a prestige route, but the later arrivals were used on other services. Service numbers were not carried, but the former front number box was fitted with a plate reading "A Cocheras" (To the Depot) which could be illuminated when the bus was on its last run at night. The trolleybuses were well

No.51 on Paseo de Pamplona, 2 February 1968. (Ray DeGroote)

No.54 at Paseo Marina, 2 February 1968. (Ray DeGroote)

cared for, but owing to a change in policy, they were gradually withdrawn, the last running on 9 October 1975. Three were acquired for preservation. Of these no.72 remains in Zaragoza livery at Ejea de los Caballeros. Nos.73 and 75 have been repainted into San Sebastian livery and the former is in the Basque Transport Museum at Azpetia, retaining the same number. No.75 is believed to be in Donostia.

Total number of double-deckers operated: 12

Of the 123 Q1s exported to Spain, only 103 actually saw service as double-deckers. Six of the others ran as single-deckers only. Two were rebuilt and ran as double-deck motorbuses. Fourteen were scrapped without seeing further service.

There were apparently plans to sell eight trolleybuses of London Transport classes N1 and N2 to an unknown overseas operator. The buses remained stored at Fulwell until 1962, long after the others of these classes had been broken up, but were then sold to George Cohen Ltd for scrapping at Colindale.

Bibliography

Els Autobusos a Barcelona. A.G. Mazip. Published by the author, Barcelona, 1996
Buses Illustrated no.72, March 1961, no.76, July 1961 and nos.116/7, November and December 1964
The Q1s in Spain. OnLine Video, 1999
London Trolleybuses Abroad. The Omnibus Society/The PSV Circle, publication no.LTB1, 1965

GERMANY

BERLIN

No conventional double-deck trolleybuses ever operated on the collection of lines which made up the separate trolleybus systems of east and west Berlin. However in 1955 the BVG (Ost) placed in service a double-deck tractor-trailer unit, of which the trailer was based on eight similar motorbuses which had been obtained some two years earlier and were themselves based on a pre-war vehicle which entered service in Dresden in 1938. The body was built by the LOWA factory at Werdau, which was responsible for the first type of standard tram of the DDR, and the tractor was built by LEW Hennigsdorf. The body part was 11.22m/36ft 6in. long and 2.4m/7ft 10in. wide. It ran on two rear axles only, the front portion being raised to accommodate the rear wheels of the tractor. Overall length, including the tractor, was 14.96m/48ft 9in. Despite adequate headroom on both decks, height was only 3.97m/13ft. The very attractive streamlined body had a rear entrance and a front exit and accessibility was excellent, there being only one step from road level to the floor of the saloon. The conductor had a fixed post at the rear and there were two straight rearwards-ascending staircases on the offside. Exit was by the front door and both entrance and exit were enclosed by outward-hung sliding doors. Seating capacity was 42/20 and 42 standees could be carried, three of these on the upper deck. Livery was cream, with a black line below the lower deck windows. The unit was classed as ES6 and numbered 2001 (tractor) and 201 (trailer). The set was used on the first trolleybus line to be operated by the BVG (Ost), O40, Ostbahnhof – Robert-Koch-Platz. No further examples were built and it was withdrawn with the closure of line O40 in December 1972.

HAMBURG

During the earlier part of the second world war, preliminary design studies had been prepared for three-axle double-deck trolleybuses which would run in Berlin, pulling double-deck trailers. These would indeed have been an impressive sight, but as the tide of war turned, the plans were shelved and, despite its fleets of double-deck motorbuses, Berlin operated only single-deck trolleybuses, with the exception mentioned above.

Across the River Elbe from Hamburg lies the formerly independent town of Harburg, which by the 1930s was served by several local tram routes in addition to one running through to the city centre. In 1937 the Hamburger Hochbahn – operator of all U-Bahn, tram and bus services in the city – decided to convert three of the local Harburg routes (32, 34 and 38) to trolleybus operation and for this ordered 24 vehicles, of which 16 would have been double-deckers. There were at this time some Büssing double-deck motorbuses entering service and the trolleybuses would presumably have been based on their design. In accordance with this plan, tram line 32 was abandoned on 30 May 1939, but as neither overhead nor vehicles were ready, it had to be replaced provisionally by a motorbus service. Owing to the outbreak of war, this "provisional" arrangement had to last for almost ten years, until single-deck trolleybuses took over

the service on 28 April 1949. The order for the 16 double-deckers was presumably cancelled. On 1 November 1950 trolleybuses replaced motorbuses on line A4 to Eissendorf/Beerentalweg, this service taking the number 04.

On 8 February 1953 this line was extended from Bahnhof Harburg to the suburb of Fleestedt, this section also being a conversion of a motorbus service. To operate on this extension, 11 single-deckers and five double-deckers were bought from Henschel of Kassel, the chassis of the double-deckers being in fact ten years old. Possibly they had been built in connexion with the plans for Berlin outlined above. All were given bodies built by Nord-Westdeutschen Fahrzeugebau of Wilhelmshaven and the double-deckers were strikingly modern in appearance. With wrap-round windows at the front of each deck, they were also very attractive and looked rather lighter than they actually were. The local newspaper, however, may have had some misgivings, since, when they were presented to the public for the first time on 8 January, wrote in its edition of the next day, that, with their height and size, they would, particularly in the narrow streets of the town centre, bring an "interesting nuance" to the local scene. With this conversion, local road transport in Harburg was entirely electrically operated.

The buses, numbered 331-335, were 10.50m/34ft 2in. long by 2.50m/8ft 2½in. wide and, with trolley booms lowered, had a height of 4.8m/15ft 6in., about .8m/2ft 8in. more than double-deck motorbuses in Germany. It would seem that trolleybuses were not covered by the same regulations as motorbuses, which were normally limited to a height of 4m/13ft. The body was laid out for passenger flow from rear to front, with a rear entrance and a central exit. Two staircases were fitted on the offside, that at the rear ascending to the rear and that behind the driver's cab ascending forwards. Seating was for 39/20 and there was standing room on the lower deck for 34 passengers. They were given the same shaped plywood

All five double-deckers laid up in 1956 and awaiting a better future in Erfurt. (W.J. Wyse, courtesy London Area, Light Rail Transit Association)

Near and off-side views of no.334 at Bahnhof Harburg, October 1953. (tramway.com collection)

A double-decker at a suburban terminus. (W.J. Wyse, courtesy London Area, Light Rail Transit Association)

seats as the class V6 trams which were then entering service. A loudspeaker system was fitted to allow the conductor to announce stops. In their attractive HHA livery of scarlet and cream, they could have passed for Londoners, but they were of vastly more advanced concept than the contemporary London Q1 trolleybuses.

On 5 May 1953 the service on which they operated was renumbered 43, the other trolleybus service becoming 41 at the same time. Unfortunately the double-deckers had very little time in which to prove themselves. On 1 November 1953 the local elections resulted in the replacement of the social-democratic city council by a conservative group known as the "Hamburg Block" and plans to convert the other two local routes to trolleybus operation were dropped, motorbuses taking over on line 42. Although planned in 1954, this was not actually put into effect until 1 October 1957. Line 44 continued to be operated by trams until a later date. Road building and development of the U-Bahn network now had

priority. Line 41 was converted to diesel buses in April 1956 and later in that year its single-deckers were transferred to line 43, the double-deckers then being taken out of service and stored. They were then sold to Erfurt in the DDR and left Hamburg under tow for that city on 5 February 1957. There were some complaints about this disposal of vehicles which had been in service for just over three years, but they went unheeded by the city authorities. After conversion to single-deck configuration, they entered service in July 1957 and ran until the abandonment of trolleybuses in Erfurt in 1975.

Bibliography

Berliner Omnibusse. Gammrath, Jung, Schmiedeke. Alba Verlag, Düsseldorf, 3rd edition, revised, October 1999
Die Strassenbahn in Harburg, ihre Vorläufer und Nachfahren Detlev Lüder. Published by the author, Hannover 1985
Nahverkehr in Hamburg. GeraNova Verlag, 2000

STATISTICS

Total numbers of double-deck trolleybuses operated, by country:

Australia	59
Malaya	5
Sri Lanka	35
Germany DDR	1
Germany BRD	5
Portugal	50
Russia	12
Spain	172
South Africa	522
Total	**861**

Total number of exports of new double-deck vehicles from Britain, by manufacturer:

AEC: Adelaide 30, Sydney 3 + 10, Johannesburg 19, Durban 13, Moscow 1,   Total 76

BUT: Colombo 35, Pretoria 10, Johannesburg 60 + 50, Barcelona 27, Cadiz 4.   Total 186

Daimler: Pretoria 18.   Total 18

Guy: Demonstrator/Cape Town 1.   Total 1

Karrier-Clough: Bloemfontein 1.   Total 1

Leyland: Durban 11 + 17, Pretoria 10, Adelaide 5, Sydney 11.   Total 54

Ransomes: Cape Town 30.   Total 30

Sigma Quest: Johannesburg 1.   Total 1

Sunbeam: Pretoria 12 + 10, Durban 11 + 12 + 52, Johannesburg 11 + 8 + 25 + 20, Cape Town 71+25.   Total 257

Total exports from Britain: 623

Total exports from Italy: Johannesburg 20, Porto 50.   Total 70

Vehicles built locally: Spain 38, Germany (DDR) 1, Germany (BRD) 5, Russia 11, South Africa 4.   Total 59

Export of second-hand vehicles from Britain: Spain 125 (of which 103 ran as double-deckers), Malaya 5.   Total 130 (108 into service)

From this it would appear that exports from Britain accounted for slightly over 70% of all double-deck trolleybuses which operated in other countries. As noted alongside, exports of single-deckers had begun just at the dawn of the trolleybus era, around the beginning of the First World War. But the export of double-deckers was a phenomenon of the 1930s, based in most cases on the perceived need to replace trams by vehicles of similar capacity. It was no doubt boosted by a strong home market and encouraged by Britain's abandonment of the gold standard in 1931. Exports of trolleybuses must have made a significant contribution to all exports of commercial vehicles at this time. Interest in the trolleybus seems to have lasted longer in some overseas cities than it did in Britain and the last British-style system was intended to open, in Colombo, in 1951 or 1952; in fact it did not do so until 1953. By that date interest in Britain had definitely begun to wane. But in the end the same forces as operated in the home market came into play and by the 1960s the double-deck trolleybus no longer had a future overseas.

Of the other countries, the Italian exports were very much in the British tradition, the vehicles built in Barcelona also followed this and were rebuilds of British motorbuses in any case. The Moscow vehicles were direct copies of the AEC trolleybus exported to Russia. The design of the Johannesburg experimental vehicles was based on contemporary British motorbuses. Only the Germans made any attempt to initiate a new design of double-deck trolleybus, with two quite different models, but the numbers were so small that these had no influence on other operators. It would seem that Sunbeam was the most prolific exporter of double-deckers and they also exported a fair number of single-deckers, although some of the other manufacturers such as AEC, which sold approximately 238 buses to Shanghai and Singapore alone at an earlier date, also did well in this field. In fact the total number of single-deckers exported from Britain, at 1378, was more than double the number of double-deckers. And, as with trams, double-deckers formed only a tiny proportion of all trolleybuses operated.

GERMAN
"ANDERTHALBDEKKERS"

A side view of one of Osnabrück's vehicles. (Müller und Ley, Würzbach)

In the early 1950s there was developed in what was then the Federal Republic of (West) Germany the concept of the one and a half deck bus. This was a vehicle, often on three axles, in which the floor of the lower deck was lowered at the rear and an upper deck, laid out in the same manner as a British lowbridge bus, was fitted over this portion. This gave a

Details of one and a half deck trolleybuses (all three axle):

Operator	Fleet nos	Built	Withdrawn	Chassis	Body
Aachen	22	1957	1972	Henschel	Ludewig
Hildesheim	12/15	1960	1969	Henschel	Ludewig*
	17-19	1960	1969	Henschel	Vetter*
	24	1961	1969	Henschel	Ludewig*
Osnabrück	209	1957	1968	Henschel	Ludewig*
	212-215	1959	1968	Henschel	Ludewig*
	201-204	1959	1968	Henschel	Ludewig*
	227-235	1960	1968	Henschel	Ludewig(1)
Wuppertal	311	1956	1971	Krupp	Ludewig(2)
	312	1957	1971	Krupp	Ludewig(2)
	309	1964	1970	Henschel	Ludewig*

*New bodies on older chassis
(1) Rebuilt as diesel buses 1968. (2) New bodies fitted 1967. Aachen 22, as rebuilt for one-person operation, is preserved in Britain at the Sandtoft Trolleybus Museum. It is not at present in running order.

With the booms lowered into the roof, this example in Hildesheim looked very like a motorbus. (Müller und Ley, Würzbach)

maximum overall height of 3.45m and thus a wider route availability than a conventional double-decker. The firm which developed the design was Ludewig GmbH of Essen, but other firms were later licensed to build the type. Most of those built for urban service were designed for passenger flow, with a large rear platform and a seated conductor. Many were later rebuilt for one-person operation and later examples were built for this. Seating capacity depended on the actual layout, but was generally in the range 27/25 and total capacity was about 25 more than in a single-decker. Until the

Osnabrück no.229 on display at the Schiene und Strasse exhibition in Essen in 1960. (B.A. Jenkins)

No.22 makes an interesting contrast with Teesside RTB no.2 at Sandtoft in August 2003. (Author)

mid-1960s, the design proved extremely popular with both urban operators and some were also built as coaches. A few remain in service to-day.

As this period was also that of maximum popularity of the trolleybus in the Federal Republic, it was not surprising that some operators would want to have trolleybuses to this design. Beginning with Wuppertaler Stadtwerke in 1956, Ludewig supplied a total of 25 trolleybuses, some of these being new bodies on older chassis. The firm of Vetter, which had obtained a licence for the type in 1960, also supplied

An interior view of Aachen no.22, as preserved at the Sandtoft Museum. (Author)

One of the first two Wuppertal vehicles, no.311 or 312, in the city centre on 12 May 1958. (Noel Reed)

three trolleybuses, making a total of 28 such vehicles. The main difference from the motorbus design was that the roof of the upper deck was lowered over the forward windows to accommodate the trolley booms and a notch was cut in the sides to allow these to swing freely and also allow them to be lowered as necessary. Seating capacities varied between operators; the Aachen trolleybus, as rebuilt for one-person operation, seated 17/42.

Along with the trolleybus, the design fell from favour after the mid-1960s and the last trolleybus ran in 1971. Some, which had fairly new bodies, were converted to motorbuses.

Bibliography

Eineinhalbdeck-Omnibusse. H Hanke. Omnibusspeigel – Sonderheft 819, 1981

TWO THAT DIDN'T GET AWAY

London Transport no.1745 of class SA2, originally intended for Durban.

London Transport AEC no.1749 of class SA3, built for Johannesburg. Both views taken at Chadwell Heath on 15 September 1956. (Author)

SPECIAL OCCASIONS

Spotlessly clean, Pretoria Daimler no.174 and Sunbeam no.145 are seen on a special tour organised by the Railway Society of Southern Africa in July 1971. (Roger M. Perry)

Johannesburg's official last trolleybus, no.1649. (James Smith)

On the last morning of trolleybus service in Durban, no.2068 is seen at the junction of Bartle Road and Stellawood Road in Umbilo. (Kevan J. Mardon collection)

The line-up of Johannesburg's new double-deckers on the official opening day of the demonstration project, 4 August 1982. (John Fran, courtesy Kevan J. Mardon)

Durban no.2067 as decorated and illuminated at Christmas 1964. (Kevan J. Mardon collection)

One of Pretoria's Daimler trolleybuses, no.174, stands outside the railway station on 24 May 1970. It was waiting to take a party of members of the Railway Society of Southern Africa on a tour of the system. (Roger M. Perry)

Pretoria Sunbeam no.145 has returned to the station on conclusion of the same tour. (Roger M. Perry)

On a tour in September 1976, to commemorate the 40th anniversary of the Johannesburg trolleybus system, nos. 710, on the right, and a Brockhouse bodied BUT perform interesting manoeuvres at Parkview terminus, while a preserved London transport RT comes in on the left. (Roger M. Perry)

On 22 November 1953 the Australian Electric Traction Association organised a tour of the Kogarah system in Sydney. It was intended to use single-decker no.1 but this developed contactor troubles and no.5, then newly rebuilt, was substituted. It is seen at Sans Souci, having pulled aside to allow no.8 on a service journey to overtake. (Noel Reed)

A happy group on a tour in Pretoria, on board no.174, under the guidance of Inspector Pienar (second from left). This tour was the first occasion for some years that a trolleybus had operated in Pretoria of an evening. The tour concluded with a meal in a roadhouse, the first time a vehicle of this kind had visited a restaurant! The trolley retrievers, seen in the photograph, made it an easy matter to fly shunt no.174 into this and other locations; it was pushed out again afterwards to a point where it could retake contact with the overhead. One of the participants was James Hall and from this tour came the decision to include one of the Daimlers in the Johannesburg museum. (James Smith)

On an enthusiasts' tour in Sydney, the crew proudly display the badges which would decorate the trolleybus. (Robert Clarke collection, courtesy Noel Reed)

Sydney's last trolleybus, no.14, makes its final journey at 01.30 on 30 August 1959. (Robert Clarke collection, courtesy Noel Reed)

Having reached Marine Parade, some of the elegantly-dressed guests have alighted to admire the new system. (Kevan J. Mardon collection)

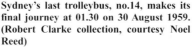

BOROUGH OF DURBAN

THE MAYOR AND TOWN COUNCILLORS

request the pleasure of the company of

At the Official Opening of the Trolley Vehicle Services on Saturday, 23rd February, 1935, at 2.30 p.m. Vehicles will convey guests over the routes, departing from the Main Police Station, West Street, at 2.30 p.m. sharp.

R.S.V.P.—THE MAYOR'S SECRETARY,
Municipal Buildings, Durban.

PRESERVATION

Fortunately the double-deck trolleybus lasted long enough in various countries to allow a few to be preserved, and these have been mentioned as appropriate in the text. These views show a few examples and also indicate the amount of work which has had to be undertaken on some of the preserved vehicles to restore them to a condition in which they can be shown to the public.

Restoration work being undertaken on Adelaide no.433 at the Tempe Bus and Truck Museum in Sydney. (John Ward Collection)

Santander-Astillero no.812 in the condition in which it was returned to Sandtoft Museum, seen at the Museum in 1978. It has now been fully restored to its original condition as LT no.1812. (Author)

A rear view of Pretoria no.177 in the James Hall Museum of Transport in Johannesburg in 1977. The trolley retrievers, unusual for a British-style trolleybus, can be clearly seen. Ahead is a preserved London Transport RT and the rear platform of Durban no.59 can just be glimpsed to the left. (Author)

Ex-Porto no.140 operating at the Sandtoft Museum in August 2003. (Author)

Durban no.59 as restored, in its home city. Apart from the Guy demonstrator of 1930, this is the only South African trolleybus to have operated on more than one system. (John Grant-Silver)

Preservation of a different kind! A Cape Town trolleybus in service as a refreshment bar at a cricket ground in 1977. According to the bi-lingual scrawl on and around the cab door, it offered cheap drinks and snacks. Although then still in fair condition, it has unfortunately not survived. (Author)

The Sydney double-deckers, unwanted, after the end of service in 1959. (Noel Reed)

The preserved Sydney trolleybus no.19 in the museum of the Southern Pacific Electric Railway at Loftus. (Author)

SUMMARY OF DISPOSAL OF LONDON TRANSPORT Q1 TROLLEYBUSES

First batch		
LT number	System	New number
1765	A Coruña	39
1766	C-Carballo	22
1767	C-Carballo	25
1768	Preserved by the LT Museum	
1769	C-Carballo	23
1770	" "	20
1771	" "	Spares
1772	" "	21
1773	" "	26
1774	" "	24
1775	S-Astillero	7
1776	Pontevedra	xx
1777	A Coruña	43(s)
1778	" "	45(s)
1779	Zaragoza	51
1780	A Coruña	37
1781	S-Astillero	9
1782	A Coruña	34
1783	" "	31
1784	" "	50(s)
1785	" "	32
1786	Zaragoza	52
1787	Vigo	xx
1788	A Coruña	49
1789	Vigo, then sold to A Coruña, number unknown	
1790	Vigo	xx
1791	Pontevedra	102
1792	Tarragona	T86
1793	" "	T87
1794	A Coruña	28
1795	" "	42
1796	" "	46(s)
1797	Vigo	xx
1798	"	xx
1799	Pontevedra	xx
1800	A Coruña	47(s)
1801	Pontevedra	105
1802	A Coruña	30
1803	" "	41
1804	Pontevedra	xx
1805	A Coruña	29
1806	Vigo	xx
1807	A Coruña	44
1808	" "	24
1809	" "	23
1810	S-Astillero	10
1811	Pontevedra	103
1812	S-Astillero	8
1813	Vigo	xx
1814	"	xx
1815	A Coruña	40(s)
1816	Pontevedra	104

First batch		
LT number	System	New number
1817	A Coruña	33
1818	Zaragoza	53
1819	A Coruña	25
1820	A Coruña	35
1821	S-Astillero	6
1822	A Coruña	26
1823	" "	27
1824	Pontevedra	101
1825	A Coruña	48
1826	" "	36
1827	Vigo	xx
1828	A Coruña	38(s)
1829	S-Astillero	11
1830	Vigo	xx
1831	"	xx
1832	Zaragoza	54
1833	" "	55
1834	" "	56
1835	" "	71
1836	" "	72
1837	" "	73
1838	" "	74
1839	" "	75
1840	" "	76
1841	? Broken up in London	

(s) Converted to single-deck
xx = no fleet number allocated

Second batch
Even numbers 1842-1890 became, in order, San Sebastian 81, 94, 80, 91, 95, 82, 72, 78, 90, 83, 79, 74, 87, 84, 73, 77, 89, 92, 88, 85, 75, 86, 92, 71, 76.
Odd numbers 1843-1891 became, in the same order, Bilbao 843-891, nos.877 and 887 being rebuilt as motorbuses.

Apart from the previously mentioned vehicles, British-style single-deckers, for use in left-hand traffic, were exported to the following cities:

Shanghai, Singapore, Kyoto, Auckland, Christchurch, Dunedin, New Plymouth, Wellington, Brisbane, Hobart, Launceston, Perth (WA), Delhi, Port of Spain, Rangoon.

Single-deckers designed for right-hand traffic were exported to the following cities:

Arnhem, Groningen, (Netherlands), Odense, Copenhagen, Hellerup (NESA) (Denmark), Edmonton, Montréal, (Canada), Donostia, Madrid, Pontevedra, Zaragoza, (Spain), Coimbra, (Portugal), Medellin, (Colombia), Sào Paulo, (Brasil), Montevideo, (Uruguay), Drammen, (Norway), Desezano, Milan, Turin, (Italy), Antwerpen, Etterbeek, Liège, (Belgium), Poznan/Posen (Poland).

More Transport Titles in the Adam Gordon Collection

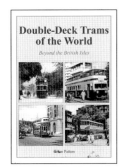

Double Deck Trams of the World, Beyond the British Isles

Brian Patton, A4 softback, 180pp, covers coloured both sides, £18.

"Patton has searched far and wide for his material, down to the photographic record of the only double-decker ever to run in Zurich. The date of operation was I April 1912 and even the reputedly dour Swiss have a sense of humour, I suspect." [Tramfare] "The illustrations are well reproduced and include some fascinating, animated views from the impressive but seldom-illustrated collection of Pam Eaton. This book endeavours to be a complete survey of overseas double-deck electric cars and necessarily only an overview of other means of propulsion, but it is unlikely ever to superseded except by an updated edition by the same author. It well merits a place on the bookshelf of any tramway student with a catholic interest in this form of design. [Tramways & Urban Transit]

Clippie

Z. Katin, a few months in the life of a tram and bus conductress in the war in Sheffield, 124pp, softback, reprint, £7

"When I was married, at the age of 22, I tried for a long time to obtain work. At the end of 18 years' interrupted effort I succeeded. The second world war had made its debut just as I had resigned myself to the knowledge that in Britain a married woman may not work outside her home except as a charlady.

Soon after my husband was called up and my son had turned 14 there came a request from the Minister of Labour and National Service that I call at the employment exchange and there be directed to work of national importance. I was not thrilled. My desire to help in the war effort was tinged with a resentment that society could only find work for me in a period of destruction and sudden death, and then only by resorting to organised compulsion.

At the "Labour" they told me I was a year too young to be given clerical work. "Could I join the Land Army?" I asked. Yes, I could, but I must be prepared to leave home. "That won't do, because my son is still at school." Very well, as you are a non-mobile woman, you have two alternatives left:

You can go into a factory; or
You can go into transport.

I thought of the heat, noise, electric light and airlessness of a munition factory and then I thought of the fresh air that blows from the Yorkshire moors across a tramcar platform in my city. And so I became a clippie – a tram conductress." [pp.5/6]

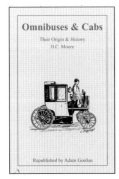

Omnibuses and Cabs – their Origin & History

H.C. Moore, reprint of 1901 publication, hardback, green cloth, dust wrapper, 282pp, 31 illustrations, £25

12 chapters devoted to omnibuses, from their origins in Paris in 1662. 2 chapters devoted to the rise and fall of Shillibeer. Other topics: the steam omnibus, the equirotal omnibus, Thomas Tilling, London General Omnibus Company, London Road Car Company, an electric omnibus, the well- conducted conductor and the ill-conducted conductor, fat and thin passengers, skid-men, ticket systems, the "corridor 'bus", "Jumpers", "Spots", pirate omnibuses - their history and tricks, etc.

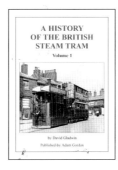

A History of the British Steam Tram

David Gladwin. Hardback, B4, 180pp inc. covers, £40. Print-run limited to 650.

Chapter titles are: Preamble [the social scene]; 1870 and All That [legislation, and early steam buses]; Trams and Traps ["workers versus wealth", The Birmingham & Aston Tramways and local opposition]; Pros and Cons – and Early Days [analysis of problems in the early days of steam, highlighting the Birmingham area]; Travails of a tram engine [study of the mechanics of tram engines, and also of the composition of rails and the effects of wheels thereon]; Manufacturers [the principal players: Wilkinson, Beyer Peacock, Black Hawthorn, Thomas Green, Hughes/Falcon/Brush, Kitson, Manning Wardle, and Merryweather]; Digressions [odd-bods (smaller manufacturers + non-steam engines): Mékarski, Brunner, Dick Kerr, Fireless, Fox Walker, Franco-Belge, Grantham, Hydroleum, Krauss, Matthews, Prima Donna, Serpollet, SNCF, Telford, Winterthur, and Woods]; People Carriers [principal trailer manufacturers, including walk-round tour of the Britannia Works of Brown Marshalls]; Lifeguards and Lights [mostly lifeguards and patents]; Permanent Way [fascinating step by step account of how the PW is laid, detailing the essential tools, as seen through the eyes of an apprentice].

Toy and Model Trams of the World, Volume 1

Gottfried Kuře and David Voice, 128pp, A4, all colour, £25.

[Back cover comment]: "Following a lifetime of modelling and collecting small trams (the authors) have teamed up to pool their knowledge in this definitive work describing toy and model trams, trolleybuses and underground trains from over the whole world. In volume I the authors look at toy trams, all die cast small trams and the vast souvenir market. The book gives invaluable tips about collecting and looking after toy trams, then covers historical tinplate, tinplate after 1950, wood, card, die cast, plastic, all other materials, souvenirs and children's toys. To help identify items there is a manufacturers' index and around 400 illustrations, mainly full colour photographs. Over 1,800 individual small trams, trolleybuses and underground trains are included and there are around 480 manufacturers' names, most entries having an historical summary. The book also guides the collector with market price estimates for toy trams no longer in production."

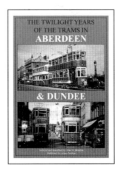

The Twilight Years of the Trams in Aberdeen and Dundee

Softback, 120pp, 231 illustrations, mostly coloured, with captions and Introduction by Alan Brotchie, £25

Includes photographs from 30 different sources.

"Congratulations on the high quality of printing and production. Very impressive." [AG, Bradford]

"This volume follows the style and the standard of earlier works on the Glasgow and Edinburgh trams and, hard though it may be to believe, surpasses those earlier works. The first impression is of fantastic quality in the reproduction of the photographs..." [TMS Journal]

INDEX

First page reference numbers to countries and towns

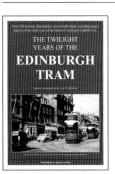

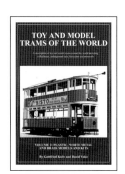